The World Wide Web F

Microsoft®
Internet Explorer 6
Illustrated Brief

Sasha Vodnik ◆ Donald I. Barker

**COURSE
TECHNOLOGY**

THOMSON LEARNING

Australia • Canada • Mexico • Singapore • Spain • United Kingdom • United States

COURSE
TECHNOLOGY

THOMSON LEARNING

The World Wide Web Featuring Microsoft® Internet Explorer 6 - Illustrated Brief

Sasha Vodnik/Donald I. Barker

Managing Editor:
Nicole Jones Pinard

Senior Product Manager:
Emily Heberlein

Associate Product Manager:
Christina Kling Garrett

Production Editor:
Daphne Barbas

Developmental Editor:
Jeanne Herring

Editorial Assistant:
Elizabeth M. Harris

QA Manuscript Reviewers:
Danielle Shaw, Chris Scriver

Text Designer:
Joseph Lee, Black Fish Design

Composition House:
GEX Publishing Services

The Illustrated Series Vision

Teaching and writing about computer applications and the Internet can be extremely rewarding and challenging. How do we engage students and keep their interest? How do we teach them skills that they can easily apply on the job? As we set out to write this book, our goals were to develop a textbook that:

- ▶ works for a beginning student
- ▶ provides varied, flexible and meaningful exercises and projects to reinforce the skills
- ▶ stays current with the quickly changing World Wide Web
- ▶ serves as a reference tool
- ▶ makes your job as an educator easier, by providing resources above and beyond the textbook to help you teach your course

Our popular, streamlined format is based on advice from instructional designers and customers. This flexible design presents each lesson on a two-page spread, with step-by-step instructions on the left, and screen illustrations on the right. This signature style, coupled with high-caliber content, provides a comprehensive yet manageable introduction to Microsoft Internet Explorer 6 — it is a teaching package for the instructor and a learning experience for the student.

ACKNOWLEDGMENTS

Thanks to Jeanne Herring, my developmental editor; because of the fresh perspective she lent my writing and her advice on approaching the tough sections, the final shape of this book owes her much. Thanks to Emily Heberlein, this book's product manager, who kept all of us informed and on-track across multiple time zones. Thanks to Em Phasis and Tom Ace for technical consultations. Thanks to my parents, Diana and Jim Vodnik, for unfailing life-long love and support. Thanks to Dylan Tierney for his pasta e fagioli. Thanks to Jan Nathan Long for good grace on nights I had to burn the midnight oil. Finally, thanks to Gracie for getting me out of the house during long days at the computer.

Sasha Vodnik

Creating a book is a team effort: I would like to thank Nicole Pinard, for publishing the book; Emily Heberlein, for managing the project; and Jeanne Herring, for developmental guidance. Special thanks to the production, editorial, and marketing staff for all their hard work. Finally, I'm forever grateful to Chia-Ling, Melissa, Irick, and Verlyn, for their patience, understanding, support, and unwavering love.

Don Barker

Preface

Welcome to *Microsoft Internet Explorer 6– Illustrated Brief.* Each lesson in the book contains elements pictured to the right in the sample two-page spread.

► How is the book organized?

The book is organized into four units on Internet Explorer, covering how to use Internet Explorer to navigate, search, and explore the Web.

► What kinds of assignments are included in the book? At what level of difficulty?

The assignments on the blue pages at the end of each unit increase in difficulty. Case studies provide a variety of interesting and relevant business applications for skills. Assignments include:

- **Concepts Reviews** include multiple choice, matching, and screen identification questions.

- **Skills Reviews** provide additional hands-on, step-by-step reinforcement.

- **Independent Challenges** are case projects requiring critical thinking and application of the skills learned in the unit. The Independent Challenges increase in difficulty, with the first Independent Challenge in each unit being the easiest (most step-by-step with detailed instructions). Independent Challenges 2–4 become increasingly open-ended, requiring more independent thinking and problem solving.

- **Visual Workshops** show an existing Web page and require students to locate the page on the Web without any step-by-step guidance.

Each 2-page spread focuses on a single skill.

Concise text introduces the basic principles in the lesson and integrates the student motivation (indicated by the paintbrush icon).

Internet

Printing a Web Page

Internet Explorer enables you to print the Web page displayed in your document window. Printing a Web page can be useful if you find information that you'd like to review later, away from your computer. It also allows you to easily share information you find on the Web with friends and associates. Practice printing in Internet Explorer by printing the home page.

Steps

QuickTip

You can also print a Web page by clicking the Print button on the Standard Buttons toolbar; however, this shortcut prints a page using the default settings, without allowing you to customize the print job.

1. **Click File on the menu bar, then click Print Preview**
   The Print Preview window opens, as shown in Figure A-12. The Print Preview function creates a mock-up of how the current Web page will appear when printed. Print Preview can be helpful in determining how a Web page will appear when printed, how many pages a printed document will take, and whether or not color elements will print on a single-color printer. Note that some graphic and color elements may not appear on the printout, depending on your printer's resolution and whether or not it prints in color.

2. **Click Close to close the Print Preview window**

3. **Click File on the menu bar, then click Print**
   The Print dialog box opens, as shown in Figure A-13. Table A-5 describes the Internet Explorer printing options. You may see additional tabs in your Print dialog box, depending on the printer connected to your computer.

4. **Click OK**
   The Print dialog box closes, and the current Web page prints. If you are not connected to a printer, or if the printer fails to work, ask your technical support person or instructor for assistance.

TABLE A-5: Printing options

tab	option	description
General	Select Printer	Displays information about the active printer
	Page Range	Indicates the pages to print
	Number of copies	Specifies how many copies to print
	Collate	Prints multiple copies of the document in sequence
Options	Print frames	Displays options for how frames are printed
	Print all linked documents	Prints the selected area as well as the contents of each page for which a link exists in the selected area
	Print table of links	Prints the selected area as well as a table listing all links located in the selected area

Hints as well as troubleshooting advice, right where you need them – next to the step itself.

Quickly accessible summaries of key terms, toolbar buttons, or keyboard alternatives connected with the lesson material. Students can refer easily to this information when working on their own projects at a later time.

Every lesson features large, full-color representations of what the screen should look like as students complete the numbered steps.

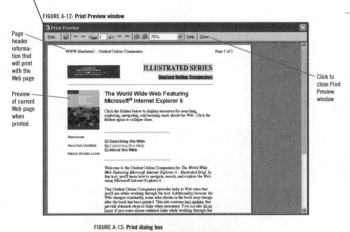

FIGURE A-12: Print Preview window

Page header information that will print with the Web page

Preview of current Web page when printed

Click to close Print Preview window

FIGURE A-13: Print dialog box

Your options may vary

Printing a Help topic

You can also print information from Internet Explorer Help. With the Help topic you want to print displayed in the Help window, click the Options button, then click Print on the menu that opens. Depending on where you are in the Help index, you may then need to choose whether to print a selected topic or all of the topics under a selected heading.

The Print dialog box that opens next is exactly like the one you use to print a Web page as shown in Figure A-13. Printing a Help topic allows you to keep information that you're not sure you could easily find again; you can also use a printed Help topic to refer to a procedure without continually switching between the Help window and the browser window.

Internet

Clues to Use boxes provide concise information that either expands on the major lesson skill or describes an independent task that in some way relates to the major lesson skill.

► **What Web resources are available with this book?**

The Internet changes rapidly. In order to keep all the links featured in the book up to date, students access all of the links in the book through the Student Online Companion, located at *www.course.com/ downloads/ illustrated/ie6*. Created specifically for this book, this companion Web site contains all the links used by students plus other links for further exploration.

► **What online learning options are available to accompany this book?**

Options for this title include a testbank in WebCT and Blackboard ready formats to make assessment using one of these platforms easy to manage. Visit www.course.com for more information on our online learning materials.

Instructor Resources

The Instructor's Resource Kit (IRK) CD is Course Technology's way of putting the resources and information needed to teach and learn effectively into your hands. All the components are available on the IRK and many of the resources can be downloaded from www.course.com.

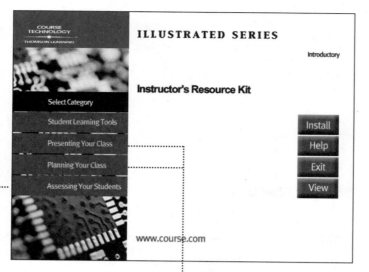

ASSESSING YOUR STUDENTS

ExamView
ExamView is a powerful testing software package that allows you to create and administer printed, computer (LAN-based), and Internet exams. ExamView includes hundreds of questions that correspond to the topics covered in this text, enabling students to generate detailed study guides that include page references for further review. The computer-based and Internet testing components allow students to take exams at their computers, and also save you time by grading each exam automatically.

PRESENTING YOUR CLASS

Figure Files
Figure Files contain all the figures from the book in .bmp format. Use the figure files to create transparency masters or in a PowerPoint presentation.

PLANNING YOUR CLASS

Instructor's Manual
Available as an electronic file, the Instructor's Manual is quality-assurance tested and includes unit overviews, detailed lecture topics for each unit with teaching tips, comprehensive sample solutions to all lessons and end-of-unit material, and extra Independent Challenges. The Instructor's Manual is available on the Instructor's Resource Kit CD-ROM, or you can download it from www.course.com.

Sample Syllabus
Prepare and customize your course easily using this sample course outline (available on the Instructor's Resource Kit CD-ROM).

Contents

Internet

Read This Before You Begin

Software Information and Required Installation

This book was written using Microsoft Internet Explorer 6.0 with a typical installation of Microsoft Windows XP. All of the steps and exercises have been tested using Internet Explorer 6.0 with both Microsoft Windows XP and Microsoft Windows 2000.

What is the Student Online Companion?

Units B, C, and D of this book are integrated with the Student Online Companion (SOC), a Web-based resource that contains the links necessary to work through the units. The SOC also contains any updates to steps or other content since the book was published; therefore, it's important to check the SOC before beginning each unit. To open the Student Online Companion, go to the following URL: *www.course.com/downloads/illustrated/ie6*.

If you are using your own computer, or if your computer lab allows you to make such changes, you can set the SOC home page as your browser home page by following these steps:

1. Open the Student Online Companion

2. Click **Tools** on the menu bar, then click **Internet Options**

3. Click the **Use Current button**, then click **OK**

For more information on setting a home page, see the Clues to Use box on page B-7.

If setting the SOC as your browser home page is not an option, you can instead make the SOC easily accessible by adding its URL to your list of Favorites (again, if you are using your own computer or your computer lab allows it). To create this Favorite:

1. Open the Student Online Companion

2. Click **Favorites** on the menu bar, then click **Add to Favorites**

3. Click **OK**

For more information on creating and using Favorites, see page B-12.

If you choose not to change your home page or add a Favorite, you can still easily complete all of the steps. Each unit and practice section includes the URL for the Student Online Companion.

Why is my screen different from the book?

1. The toolbars and buttons in your browser window may be different if you are using an operating system other than Microsoft Windows XP.

2. Figures throughout the book show the Student Online Companion (SOC) home page as the browser home page. If the computer you are working on has a different browser home page, your screen will look different. You can work through the steps without a problem no matter what Web page is set as your browser home page. (See above for instructions on how to set the Student Online Companion home page as your browser home page.)

Internet

Getting
Started with the World Wide Web

Objectives

- ► **Understand the Internet**
- ► **Understand Microsoft Internet Explorer 6**
- ► **Start Internet Explorer**
- ► **Investigate the Internet Explorer window**
- ► **Work with menus and toolbars**
- ► **Move around a Web page**
- ► **Get Help**
- ► **Print a Web page**
- ► **Exit Internet Explorer**

This unit introduces the Internet, the World Wide Web, and Microsoft Internet Explorer browsing software and add-ons. As you become familiar with Internet Explorer, you will discover it provides many useful tools for accessing the World Wide Web. ✐━━ In order to understand the World Wide Web and how to use it, you need to become familiar with the basics. You start by studying the Internet and the World Wide Web and learning how to use Internet Explorer.

Internet

Understanding the Internet

The **Internet** is a collection of networks that connects computers all over the world. A **network** consists of two or more computers that are connected to share data. The Internet connects millions of computers, using a combination of telephone lines, fiber-optic cables, satellites, and other telecommunications media, as depicted in Figure A-1. To get a feel for the varied features of the Internet, examine its main uses.

The most popular uses of the Internet include the following:

► The **Web**, short for the **World Wide Web**, is a huge collection of Internet documents that use a consistent format for easy accessibility. These documents, known as **Web pages**, often contain text and graphics and may also include audio and video files. Web pages also contain **links**, which are formatted objects that refer to other documents on the Web. Clicking a linked word, phrase, or graphic on a Web page opens another Web page containing related information. Links simplify understanding of the connections between different Web pages that are grouped together in a **Web site** and make finding relevant information on a topic of interest easier.

► **E-mail**, short for **electronic mail**, enables users to send messages to other users via an Internet connection. Each user has a unique name, known as an **e-mail address**. In addition to text, e-mail messages can include graphics, as well as attachments of other files. E-mail serves a function similar to that of the U.S. Postal Service, in terms of delivering messages and information from one address to another address or addresses; but messages can be delivered in a matter of seconds or minutes, rather than days.

► **Newsgroups** (also referred to as **Usenet**) are online forums where users can read and post messages on a variety of subjects. Unlike e-mail, where messages are sent from a single user to one or more addressees, a newsgroup message is sent to a location on the Internet where anyone can access and read it. Responses to that message are posted next to the original message, making it easy to read input from multiple people on a given idea. A similar feature, the **message board**, allows reading and posting by a limited audience of Internet users, such as employees of an organization or members of a group.

► **Instant messaging** is a communication system that transmits text messages between individual Internet users almost instantaneously. These messages, known as **instant messages**, or **IMs**, are limited to text. The advantage of instant messaging is that it functions even faster than e-mail. Unlike e-mail, however, an instant message can be delivered only if the recipient is online at the same time as the sender. In addition, all Internet users do not share a single system for instant messages.

► **File sharing** is a technology that allows Internet users to make electronic files available for other users to browse and copy. File sharing services such as Napster, Bear Share, and Gnutella allow users to share files such as digital music, computer programs, and video clips. These services may change the way such files are typically distributed and paid for, since they eliminate the need for distribution companies to duplicate and sell items such as music and software CDs. However, the fact that file sharing systems lack a standard mechanism for paying fees to copyright holders has made such systems controversial.

FIGURE A-1: Structure of the Internet

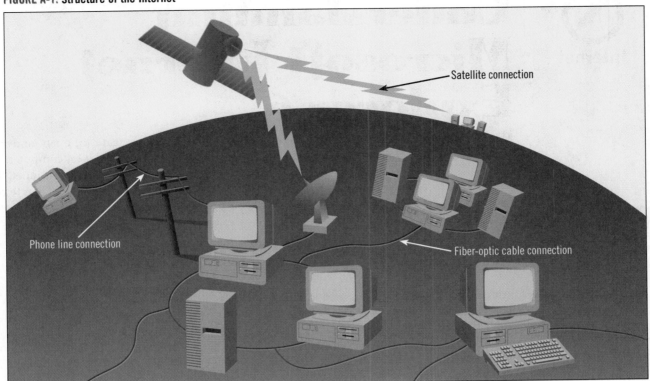

Satellite connection

Phone line connection

Fiber-optic cable connection

CLUES TO USE

Understanding intranets

An **intranet** uses the same communications technology as the Internet, but access is available only to the members of a particular company or group. Intranets offer organizations many advantages, such as additional security beyond that available on the Internet, inexpensive and easier installation and maintenance than traditional information systems, and the same familiar Web browser interface that people already use to access information on the Internet. Additionally, an intranet enables the quick distribution of information to employees at disparate locations. As a consequence, many larger corporations and organizations use intranets to distribute and share information among employees.

Internet

Internet

Understanding Microsoft Internet Explorer 6

Microsoft Internet Explorer 6 is a program that allows you to navigate to, open, and view documents. In addition to accessing different kinds of documents on your local computer, you can use Internet Explorer to browse information on the Internet or within an intranet. The Internet Explorer browser also comes with Outlook Express, a program that enables you to read e-mail and newsgroup messages. As you prepare to start using the Web, review the capabilities and functions of Microsoft Internet Explorer 6 and Outlook Express.

Details

Internet Explorer includes the following features:

Trouble?

Your Internet Explorer window may differ from the one shown in Figure A-2 if you are using an operating system other than Microsoft Windows XP.

▶ **Internet Explorer,** a program known as a **Web browser,** lets you interact with the World Wide Web. Internet Explorer 6 enables you to find, load, view, and interact with Web pages. These pages typically incorporate both text and graphics, as shown in Figure A-2; they also may include multimedia, such as sound and video clips, as shown in Figure A-3. Internet Explorer allows you to keep track of Web sites to which you want to return, as well as to easily access sites you've recently visited.

▶ **Outlook Express,** a combined e-mail program and newsgroup reader, enables you to send and receive messages and participate in newsgroup discussions. Outlook Express downloads e-mail messages from your account on the Internet, enabling you to read them even when you're not online. Outlook Express also allows you to create folders in order to save and organize messages that you don't want to delete. In addition to viewing newsgroups in Outlook Express, you can choose to download message content while you're online and then view newsgroup messages when you're no longer connected to the Internet.

FIGURE A-2: Web page containing text and graphics

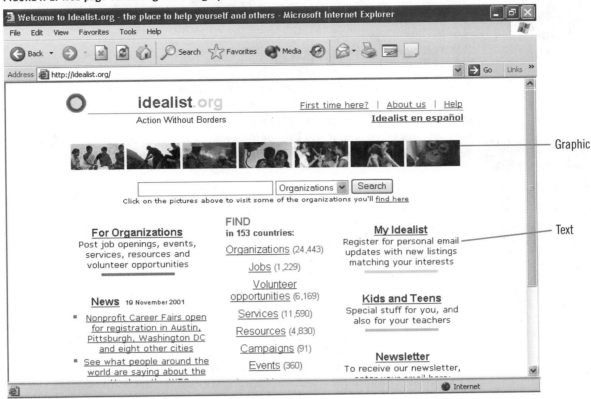

Graphic

Text

FIGURE A-3: Web page containing audio and video links

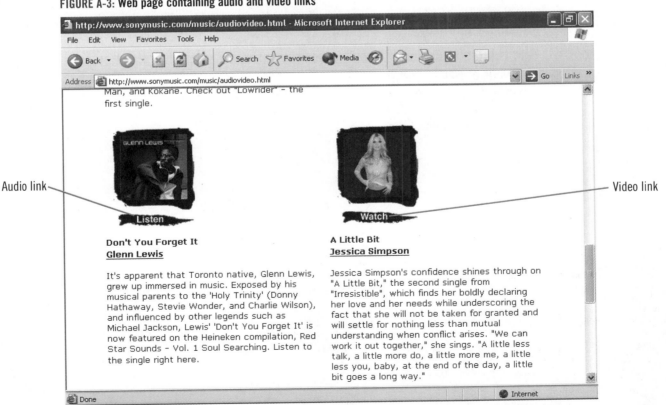

Audio link

Video link

Internet

Starting Internet Explorer

To begin using Internet Explorer, you simply click the program icon to start it. The exact location and name of the icon may vary on different computers. Hence, the steps you take to start Internet Explorer might differ from those given below. Ask your instructor or technical support person for help if you cannot locate the Internet Explorer icon. ▬▬▬ Begin learning about Internet Explorer by starting it and investigating its features.

Trouble?

Your computer screen may differ if you are using an operating system other than Microsoft Windows XP.

1. Click the **Start button**, then locate the **Internet Explorer button** 🌐

Figure A-4 shows the Internet Explorer button on the Start menu, as well as other common locations. Table A-1 describes other common methods for starting Internet Explorer. If you do not see the Internet Explorer icon on your Start menu, look for it in the locations shown in Figure A-4. If you do not see the icon in any of these places, ask your instructor or technical support person for help.

Trouble?

Your home page may differ from that shown in Figure A-5.

2. Click 🌐

If you are using the Internet Explorer icon on the desktop, you need to double-click the icon to open Internet Explorer. Internet Explorer opens and the **home page** appears, as shown in Figure A-5. The home page is the first Web page that Internet Explorer loads when you start the program. A home page is selected by default when the browser is installed, and may vary depending on who provided the software. You can also set your own home page; this process is explained in Unit B on page B-7. The figures in this book show a browser using the Student Online Companion for this book as its home page; your home page might be different. The **Student Online Companion (SOC)** is a Web page that provides links and other information you will use as you complete the steps in this book. The SOC is on the Web at *http://www.course.com/downloads/illustrated/ie6*. See the Read This Before You Begin page for more information.

3. If Internet Explorer doesn't cover the entire desktop, click the **Maximize button** on your browser window

Clicking the Maximize button expands the size of the browser window to cover all the area available on your desktop. Clicking the Minimize button reduces the browser window to a button on the taskbar.

TABLE A-1: Common ways to start Internet Explorer 6

method	steps
Taskbar button	Click the Internet Explorer button on the taskbar
Desktop icon	Double-click the Internet Explorer icon on the desktop
Start menu	Click the Start button, then click Internet Explorer
	or
	Click the Start button, point to All Programs or Programs, and then click Internet Explorer

FIGURE A-4: Common locations of the Internet Explorer icon

Icon on the desktop

Button on the Start menu

Button on the taskbar

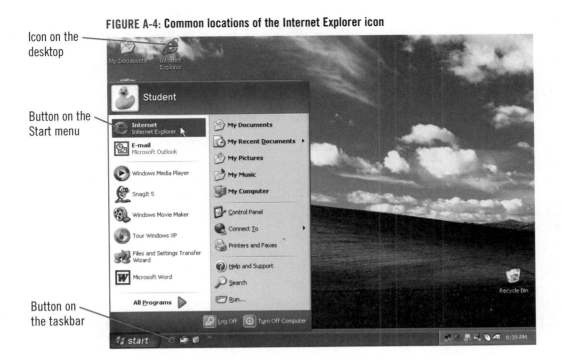

FIGURE A-5: Home page

Maximize or Restore button

Minimize button

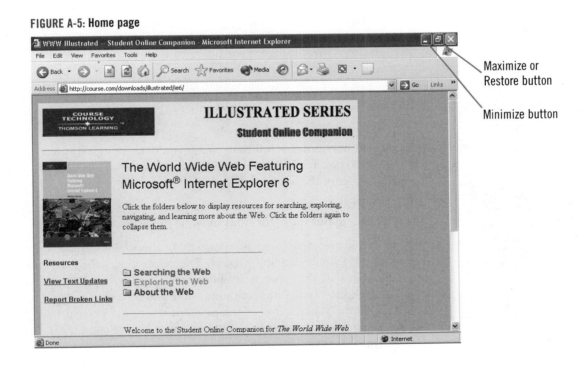

Internet

Internet

Investigating the Internet Explorer Window

When you start Internet Explorer, the Internet Explorer program window opens. The screen elements in this window enable you to view, enter, and search for information. As you investigate the Internet Explorer environment, use Figure A-6 as a guide to help you locate each of the following window elements on your screen:

Details

▶ A **Web page** is a specially formatted file designed for use on the World Wide Web. Anyone with access to the Web can view this page. A Web page typically includes text, graphics, and links that, when clicked, connect you to other Web pages. It might also include audio and video clips that you can access if your computer has the appropriate hardware and software. The **title bar** displays the title of the current Web page. The area of the browser that a Web page appears in is called the **document window**.

▶ The **menu bar** displays the names of the menus that contain Internet Explorer commands. When you click the name of a menu on the menu bar, Internet Explorer displays a list (menu) of commands from which you can choose.

▶ The **Standard Buttons toolbar** includes shortcuts to activate frequently used menu commands and navigation aids. It displays the primary navigational buttons used to move around the Web (such as Back, Forward, and Stop). You can customize the Standard Buttons toolbar.

▶ The **Address Bar** shows the current Web page address and allows the entry or selection of another Web page to view. The **Address text box** displays the address of the page shown in the document window. A **Web address**, or **Uniform Resource Locator (URL)**, is a unique string of characters that identifies the location of a Web page on the World Wide Web. You can type a Web page's URL in the Address text box and then click the **Go button** to open the page.

Trouble?

Your Links toolbar may be empty or may contain different buttons than those shown in Figure A-6.

▶ The **Links toolbar** contains a set of buttons that you can customize to quickly access Web pages that you use often.

▶ The **vertical and horizontal scroll bars** enable you to move quickly around a Web page you are viewing. The scroll box in each scroll bar indicates your relative position on the page. You may see both, one, or neither of the scroll bars, depending on the dimensions of the page you are viewing.

Trouble?

Because some companies that distribute Internet Explorer are licensed to substitute their own logos for the status indicator, your status indicator may be different.

▶ The **status indicator** (the Internet Explorer logo) becomes animated as a new Web page is loading. When the status indicator stops moving, the page-loading process is complete.

▶ The **status bar** displays important information about the current operation, such as the progress of the Web-page-loading process. The center box, called the **progress bar**, visually indicates the status of this process by filling with a blue bar. When the loading process is complete, the blue bar reaches its maximum length and then disappears. The far right side of the status bar shows the general area of the network where the current page resides, such as My Computer (on your local machine) or Internet (on a remote computer).

FIGURE A-6: Elements of the Internet Explorer window

Title bar

Menu bar

Standard
Buttons
toolbar

Address
Bar

Links
toolbar

Web
address
or URL

Status bar

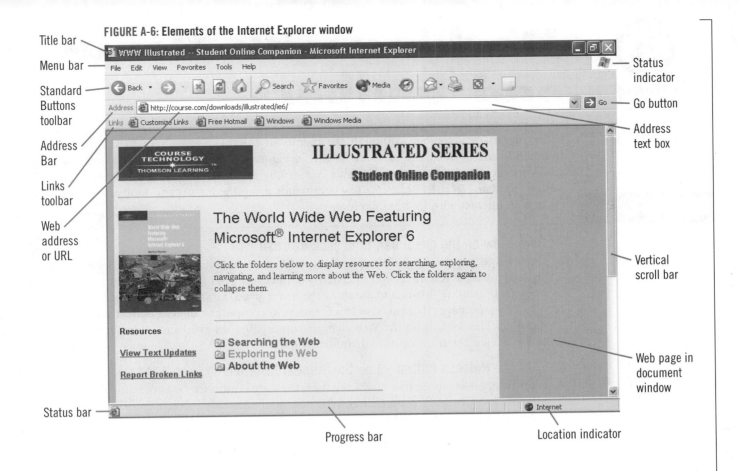

Status
indicator

Go button

Address
text box

Vertical
scroll bar

Web page in
document
window

Progress bar   Location indicator

Viewing and arranging toolbars

You can stack Internet Explorer's toolbars vertically, as shown in Figure A-6, or consolidate them into a single row, providing more room for viewing a Web page. To view a toolbar not currently visible on your screen, click View on the Menu bar, point to Toolbars, then click the name of the toolbar you would like to add. By default, the Links toolbar shares a row with the Address Bar. To expand the Links toolbar so that its icons are visible, you must first unlock the position of Internet Explorer toolbars by clicking View on the Menu bar, pointing to Toolbars, then clicking

Lock the Toolbars to uncheck it. You can then drag the Links icon down to display the toolbar fully in its own row. To redisplay the Links toolbar or Address Bar in the consolidated layout, simply drag the toolbars up into a higher row. In the consolidated display, the Address Bar, Links toolbar, and Standard Buttons toolbar share a single row, giving one or more of the toolbars the appearance of a button by default. You can drag the borders between the toolbars to change how much of each is visible.

Internet

Internet

Working with Menus and Toolbars

For many operations, Internet Explorer provides several ways to complete the same task, using either menus or a toolbar. Although the menus in Internet Explorer contain the available commands and options, the toolbars, shown in Figure A-7, offer a quicker and easier way to access frequently used commands. Table A-2 briefly describes the buttons on the Standard Buttons toolbar. ⚡ Practice a few commands using the menus and toolbars to get a feel for how to interact with Internet Explorer.

Steps 1 2 3 4

1. **Click View on the menu bar, then click Refresh**
   Refreshing, or reloading, a Web page is an important capability of a browser; it ensures that you see the most recent version of a Web page. Because your home page hasn't changed, the document window loads and displays the same page, as shown in Figure A-8. Internet Explorer saves pages that you visit in a file on your computer, called a **cache**, to reduce loading time. The content on the Web changes continually, however, and refreshing guarantees that you view the most up-to-date information.

2. **Click the Refresh button** 🔁 **on the Standard Buttons toolbar**
   If reloading takes more than a few seconds, the status indicator becomes animated and the blue bar appears in the progress bar. When the status indicator returns to a static image and the blue bar disappears, the page has successfully reloaded.

3. **Click** 🔁 **once more, this time quickly clicking the Stop button** ❌ **on the Standard Buttons toolbar before the home page finishes reloading**
   If you act quickly enough, the home page appears without graphics or other page elements. The Stop button offers a convenient way to halt the lengthy process of loading a page laden with images and other large elements, especially when you realize that the page opening is not the one you intended to open. It's especially useful when accessing the Web over a slow Internet connection, such as a modem.

4. **Click** 🔁 **once more to load the page completely**

FIGURE A-7: Internet Explorer toolbars

Standard
Buttons
toolbar

Address
Bar

Links toolbar

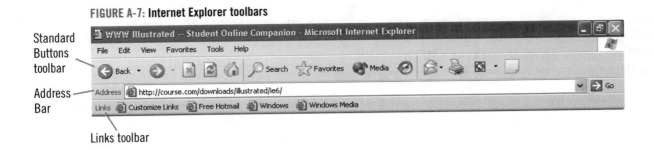

FIGURE A-8: Home page

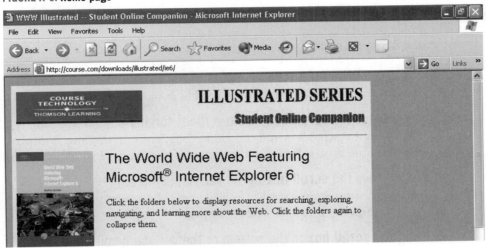

TABLE A-2: Standard Buttons toolbar buttons

button	name	description
	Back	Displays previous page
	Forward	Displays the next page in the series of pages already viewed
	Stop	Halts the page-loading process
	Refresh	Reloads a page
	Home	Displays your home (opening) page
	Search	Allows searches of the Web based on keyword(s)
	Favorites	Displays a menu of favorite Web sites from which to choose
	Media	Displays a selection of links to audio and video, along with Media Player controls
	History	Displays a menu of previously visited Web sites for quick access
	Mail	If installed, allows reading and sending of e-mail and news, along with options for either sending the Web page address or the entire page itself in an e-mail message
	Print	Prints the current Web page
	Edit	Opens the default Web page editor with the current Web page displayed and ready for modification; if Microsoft FrontPage, Microsoft Word, or another program capable of editing Web pages is installed, a different button may appear
	Discuss	Enables you to post and read messages in discussion groups that are part of some Web pages

Internet

Moving Around a Web Page

The length of a Web page depends upon the amount of content on the page. Although short and concise Web pages are generally easier to use, you will sometimes encounter pages that don't fit in the document window. Internet Explorer provides several convenient methods for moving around Web pages; Table A-3 summarizes these methods. Practice moving around your home page, using a variety of the navigation methods available in Internet Explorer.

Steps

QuickTip

You can also use the arrow keys and [Page Up] or [Page Down] to display various portions of a Web page in the document window.

1. **Click the scroll down arrow at the bottom of the vertical scroll bar**
   The document window scrolls down several lines on the home page to reveal new information at the bottom of the window.

2. **Click the scroll up arrow at the top of the vertical scroll bar**
   The document window scrolls up several lines in the home page.

3. **Click below the scroll box in the vertical scroll bar**
   The document window scrolls down the length of one window to display the next portion of your home page, stopping at the bottom if less than one window of information remains.

4. **Click above the scroll box in the vertical scroll bar**
   The document window scrolls up the length of one window, or back to the top in a short page, to show the previous view of the page.

5. **Drag the scroll box to the bottom of the vertical scroll bar**
   The document window displays the bottom of the page, as shown in Figure A-9. Notice that the scroll box has moved to the bottom of the vertical scroll bar, indicating that you have reached the end of the current Web page.

6. **Drag the scroll box to the top of the vertical scroll bar**
   The document window displays the top of the page.

7. **Press [Ctrl][End]**
   The bottom of the page appears in the document window.

8. **Press [Ctrl][Home]**
   The top of the page appears in the document window.

Finding text

Sometimes you may want to find a specific word or phrase in a Web page because you are seeking information on or mention of a particular topic. Scrolling through a Web page and trying to spot text can be a haphazard and time-consuming process. Internet Explorer provides the Find command to automate this process. To use the Find command, press [Ctrl][F], or click Edit on the Menu bar, then click Find (on this page). The Find dialog box opens. In the Find what text box, type the word or phrase you want to find, then click Find Next to locate the first occurrence of the word or phrase after your current position on the Web page. To keep searching for additional occurrences, click Find Next.

FIGURE A-9: Bottom of the home page

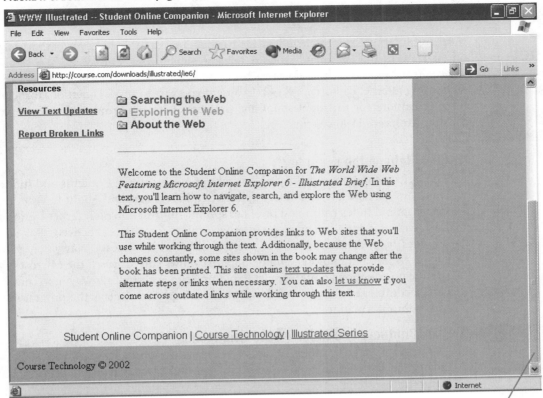

Indicates that you have reached the end of the current Web page

TABLE A-3: Methods for moving around a Web page

to move	mouse and keyboard instructions
Down several lines	Click the down arrow in the vertical scroll bar, or press [↓]
Up several lines	Click the up arrow in the vertical scroll bar, or press [↑]
Down one window	Click below the scroll box in the vertical scroll bar, or press [Page Down]
Up one window	Click above the scroll box in the vertical scroll bar, or press [Page Up]
To the top of the Web page	Drag the scroll box to the top of the vertical scroll bar, or press [Ctrl][Home]
To the bottom of the Web page	Drag the scroll box to the bottom of the vertical scroll bar, or press [Ctrl][End]

Getting Help

Microsoft Internet Explorer includes a Help system that can provide information and instructions on the features and commands you are using in the browser. This system is a valuable resource when you are uncertain about how to accomplish a task or when you encounter unexpected results while using Internet Explorer. ✎━━━ In order to prepare to answer questions that come up about Internet Explorer or to troubleshoot any problems with the browser, familiarize yourself with Internet Explorer's Help system.

Steps

1. **Click Help on the menu bar**

   The Help menu opens, displaying several options including Contents and Index, Tip of the Day, For Netscape Users, Online Support, Send Feedback, and About Internet Explorer. The Contents and Index command provides specific information on Internet Explorer. Tip of the Day gives a random hint on using Internet Explorer's features effectively. For Netscape Users provides helpful information for users familiar with Netscape Navigator, a Web browser similar to Internet Explorer. Online Support allows you to search the Microsoft Web site for specific information about Internet Explorer. Send Feedback allows you to contact Microsoft with a comment or question. About Internet Explorer displays the program's version and copyright information.

2. **Click Contents and Index on the Help menu**

   The Internet Explorer Help dialog box opens, as shown in Figure A-10. Table A-4 describes the options in the Help Topics dialog box. For now, you simply want to investigate the basic features of Explorer.

3. **Click the Customizing Your Web Browser Contents item, then click the item Correctly displaying Web pages encoded in any language from the list that appears below it**

   A description of how to view Web pages written in different languages appears in the right portion of the window, as shown in Figure A-11.

4. **Scan the information displayed in the right section of the window**

5. **When you have finished reviewing the topic, click the Close button in the upper-right corner of the Help window to close it**

   Internet Explorer appears on your desktop, with your home page displayed in the document window.

QuickTip

If an error dialog box appears when you select a Help menu command, it probably indicates that you are not currently connected to the Internet. Although the Contents and Index features are available offline (locally), other Help menu options require you to be online (that is, connected to the Internet).

FIGURE A-10: Internet Explorer Help window

Index tab

Contents tab

Currently selected Help topic

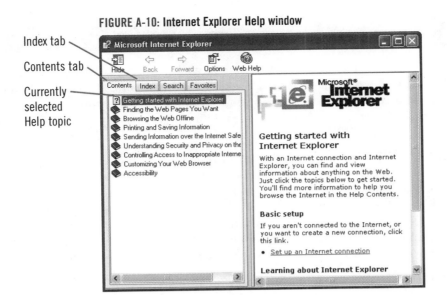

FIGURE A-11: Information on viewing Web pages in different languages

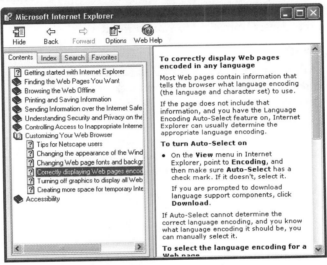

TABLE A-4: Descriptions of the Help options

option	description
Contents tab	Offers a variety of topics about Explorer to investigate
Index tab	Enables the search of Help documents by topic and keyword
Search tab	Enables the search of Help documents by keyword
Favorites tab	Enables you to maintain a list of useful or important Help topics
Hide button	Removes the tabs from view
Show button	Makes the tabs visible
Back button	Allows a return to a previously viewed Help window
Forward button	Allows a return to the next document in a series of Help windows already viewed
Options button	Opens a menu of additional options for working with the Help window
Web Help button	Provides a link to additional Help resources online

Internet

Printing a Web Page

Internet Explorer enables you to print the Web page displayed in your document window. Printing a Web page can be useful if you find information that you'd like to review later, away from your computer. It also allows you to easily share information you find on the Web with friends and associates. Practice printing in Internet Explorer by printing the home page.

QuickTip

You can also print a Web page by clicking the Print button on the Standard Buttons toolbar; however, this shortcut prints a page using the default settings, without allowing you to customize the print job.

1. Click **File** on the menu bar, then click **Print Preview**

The Print Preview window opens, as shown in Figure A-12. The Print Preview function creates a mock-up of how the current Web page will appear when printed. Print Preview can be helpful in determining how a Web page will appear when printed, how many pages a printed document will take, and whether or not color elements will print on a single-color printer. Note that some graphic and color elements may not appear on the printout, depending on your printer's resolution and whether or not it prints in color.

2. Click **Close** to close the Print Preview window

3. Click **File** on the menu bar, then click **Print**

The Print dialog box opens, as shown in Figure A-13. Table A-5 describes the Internet Explorer printing options. You may see additional tabs in your Print dialog box, depending on the printer connected to your computer.

4. Click **OK**

The Print dialog box closes, and the current Web page prints. If you are not connected to a printer, or if the printer fails to work, ask your technical support person or instructor for assistance.

TABLE A-5: Printing options

tab	option	description
General	Select Printer	Displays information about the active printer
	Page Range	Indicates the pages to print
	Number of copies	Specifies how many copies to print
	Collate	Prints multiple copies of the document in sequence
Options	Print frames	Displays options for how frames are printed
	Print all linked documents	Prints the selected area as well as the contents of each page for which a link exists in the selected area
	Print table of links	Prints the selected area as well as a table listing all links located in the selected area

FIGURE A-12: Print Preview window

Page header information that will print with the Web page

Preview of current Web page when printed

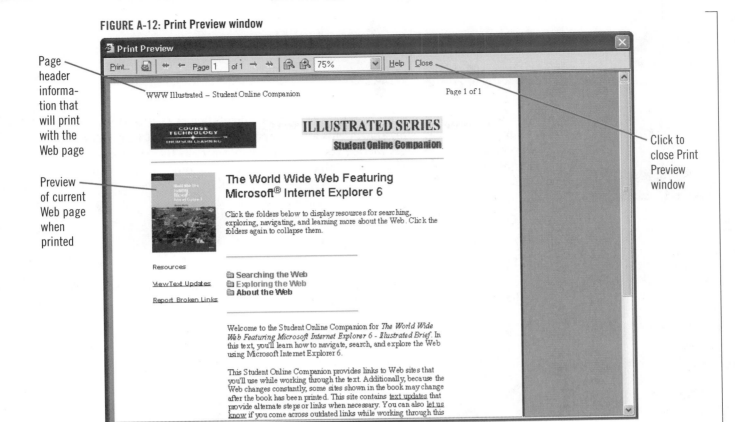

Click to close Print Preview window

FIGURE A-13: Print dialog box

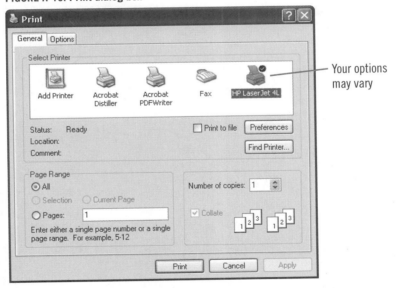

Your options may vary

Printing a Help topic

You can also print information from Internet Explorer Help. With the Help topic you want to print displayed in the Help window, click the Options button, then click Print on the menu that opens. Depending on where you are in the Help index, you may then need to choose whether to print a selected topic or all of the topics under a selected heading.

The Print dialog box that opens next is exactly like the one you use to print a Web page as shown in Figure A-13. Printing a Help topic allows you to keep information that you're not sure you could easily find again; you can also use a printed Help topic to refer to a procedure without continually switching between the Help window and the browser window.

Internet

Internet

Exiting Internet Explorer

In many other Windows programs, you need to save documents before exiting. However, a Web browser simply displays existing documents and allows the user to interact with them; it does not make changes to Web pages themselves. Therefore, you can close Internet Explorer at any time without losing data. Now that you've completed your initial investigation of Internet Explorer, exit the browser.

1. Click **File** on the menu bar

The File menu opens, as shown in Figure A-14.

2. Click **Close** on the File menu

The Internet Explorer program window closes, and you return to Windows. Table A-6 describes alternate ways to close Internet Explorer.

Opening, switching, and closing multiple instances of Internet Explorer

You can use the New, Window command on the File menu to open another instance of the Internet Explorer program. Each instance is a separate Internet Explorer window, complete with all toolbars and menus, in which you can navigate independently. Additionally, some Web pages can open additional Web pages in new Internet Explorer instances, while leaving the original page displayed in the original instance. The taskbar allows you to switch between these different instances. In some operating systems, multiple instances of the same program are grouped into a single taskbar button; you can click the button for a menu of open instances, then select the one to open. To close an instance of Explorer, use any of the methods described in Table A-6 for the instance that you want to close.

FIGURE A-14: Intenet Explorer program window with File menu open

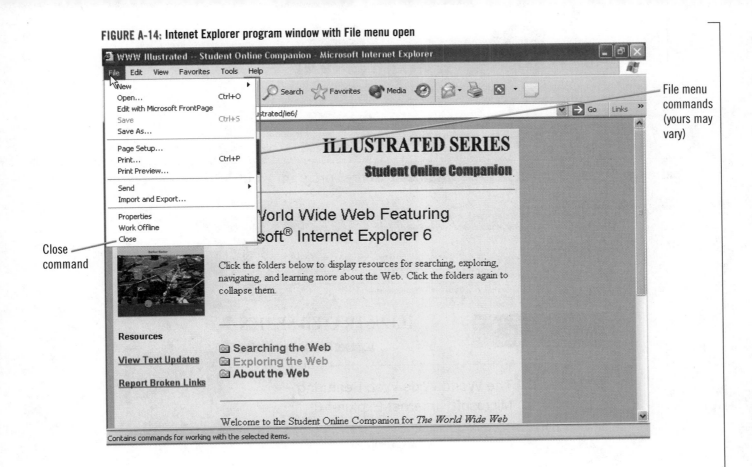

Close command

File menu commands (yours may vary)

TABLE A-6: Common methods of closing Internet Explorer

method	procedure
Menu bar	Click File on the menu bar, then click Close
Title bar button	Click the Close button on the title bar
Taskbar	Right-click the Internet Explorer program window icon on the taskbar, then click Close

Internet

Practice

► Concepts Review

Label each of the elements of the Internet Explorer program window shown in Figure A-15.

FIGURE A-15

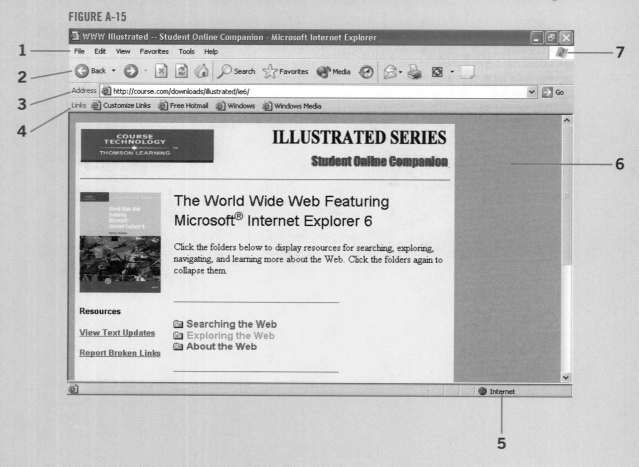

Match each of the terms below with the statement that best describes its function.

8. Standard Buttons toolbar
9. Scroll bar
10. Document window
11. Address text box
12. Status indicator

a. Contains shortcuts to menu commands
b. Displays a Web page
c. Indicates the address of the current page
d. Contains controls for moving around a document
e. Indicates Internet Explorer is loading a page

Select the best answer from the list of choices.

13. **To view another part of a Web page:**
    a. Move the scroll box in the scroll bar.
    b. Drag the toolbar.
    c. Select the Leap command from the Navigate menu.
    d. Click the Relocate button on the toolbar.

14. **To go to the top of a document:**
    a. Click the Home button on the toolbar.
    b. Drag the scroll box to the top of the scroll bar.
    c. Double-click the scroll bar.
    d. Press [Ctrl][Top].

15. **To find words in a Web page:**
    a. Press [Ctrl][F].
    b. Click the Find button.
    c. Double-click the Location toolbar.
    d. Click the Look command on the Help menu.

16. **You can access Internet Explorer Help by:**
    a. Pressing [F2].
    b. Clicking the Help button on the toolbar.
    c. Clicking Help on the menu bar.
    d. Pressing [Alt][Help].

17. **Which key(s) do you press to move down a Web page?**
    a. [Enter][End]
    b. [End]
    c. [Page Down]
    d. [Shift][End]

18. **The Standard Buttons toolbar lets you do all of the following, *except:***
    a. Print a Web page.
    b. See how much of a Web page has loaded.
    c. See a list of your favorite Web sites.
    d. Search the Web.

19. **The home page is:**
    a. A Web page devoted to the realty business.
    b. A Web page detailing information about your computer.
    c. A page you must create yourself.
    d. The initial Web page that Internet Explorer loads whenever you start the program.

20. **URL stands for:**
    a. Universal Regional Locator
    b. Uniform Resource List
    c. Universal Requester List
    d. Uniform Resource Locator

21. **You can exit Internet Explorer by:**
    a. Clicking Done on the File menu.
    b. Clicking Done on the Go menu.
    c. Clicking the Internet Explorer Close button.
    d. All of the above.

Internet

Skills Review

1. **Start Internet Explorer and identify elements of the program window.**
   a. Make sure the computer is on and Windows is running.
   b. Click the Internet Explorer button on the taskbar.
   c. Without referring to the lesson material, identify the toolbar areas, the Address Bar, the menu bar, the scroll bars, the Address text box, the status indicator, and the progress bar in the Internet Explorer program window.

2. **Move around the document window.**
   a. Click the scroll down arrow in the vertical scroll bar twice.
   b. Click the scroll up arrow on the vertical scroll bar twice.
   c. Click below the scroll box in the vertical scroll bar.
   d. Click above the scroll box in the vertical scroll bar.
   e. Drag the scroll box to the bottom of the vertical scroll bar.

3. **Explore Internet Explorer Help.**
   a. Click Help on the menu bar.
   b. Click the Contents and Index command on the Help menu.
   c. Click the Index tab, and then if necessary, click in the text box above the list that appears.
   d. Type **Viewing Web pages**, click one of the topics that appears in the box below, then click the Display button.
   e. Read the information displayed on the right side of the screen, then close the Help window.

4. **Print a Web page and exit Internet Explorer.**
   a. Click File on the menu bar, then click Print Preview.
   b. Close the Print Preview screen.
   c. Click the Print button.
   d. When the page is printed, click File on the menu bar, then click Close.

▶ Independent Challenge 1

Write a short essay on what you hope to learn from this book. Include a description of how you think the World Wide Web will help you in your academic or professional life. You can use any word processor to write and print this essay. If you are not sure if you have a word processor, use Notepad or WordPad, simple text processors included with Microsoft Windows in the Accessories program group. Be sure to type your name on the document before printing.

▶ Independent Challenge 2

You are working with a public service group that encourages people to research products they plan to buy, and the businesses that make them, before making a purchase. You have read about the Web and electronic commerce and want to find out how this can help your agency fulfill its mission. Use your library to find several recent articles on how the World Wide Web is affecting businesses, including at least one article on electronic commerce. Write a brief summary of the articles. You can use any word processor to write and print the summary. If you are not sure if you have a word processor, use Notepad or Wordpad, simple text processors included with Microsoft Windows in the Accessories program group. Be sure to type your name on the document before printing.

Internet

▶ Visual Workshop

Use the skills you learned in this unit to display the "Using secure Internet sites for transactions" topic in the Help window, as shown in Figure A-16. Print a copy of this page.

FIGURE A-16

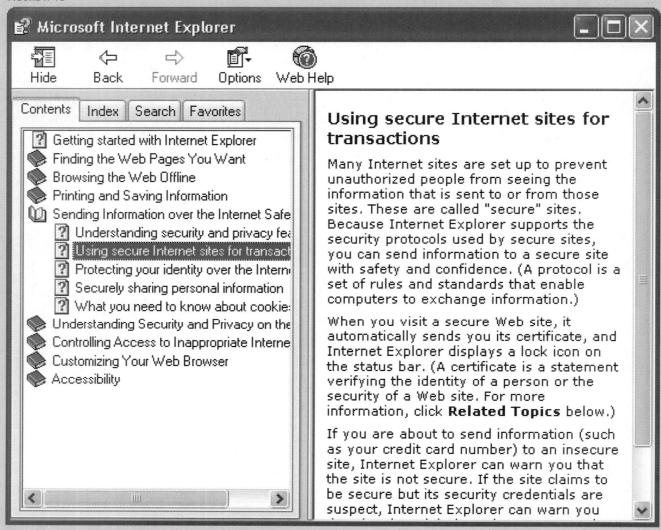

Navigating
the Web

Objectives

- ► **Understand links and URLs**
- ► **Enter a URL**
- ► **Find, start, and stop links**
- ► **Move backward and forward**
- ► **View History**
- ► **Use Favorites**
- ► **Work with navigation tools**
- ► **Understand security issues**

Once you are familiar with Internet Explorer's toolbars, menus, dialog boxes, and Help system, you are ready to navigate the Web. This unit introduces you to the basic techniques for moving between Web pages using Internet Explorer. In addition to using different methods to open a Web page, you will return to pages you have already viewed and add a page to your list of favorite pages for easy access. ✐ As you learn the basics of using Internet Explorer, you need to practice interacting with the browser and to become familiar with Internet Explorer's navigation features. Building these skills is the first step in becoming adept at moving around the Web.

Internet

Understanding Links and URLs

Like a conventional reference resource such as an encyclopedia, the World Wide Web is composed of a large number of pages filled with all sorts of information. Like an encyclopedia entry that ends with cross-references, a Web page can contain links that refer users to related Web pages. **Links**, sometimes called **hyperlinks** or **hypertext links**, are Web page elements that you can click to open other Web pages. You can use links to follow a topic from page to page through the Web, without regard to where or in what order the pages reside. To distinguish them from the other text in a Web page, links are highlighted in a special color and underlined. Figure B-1 shows a Web page featuring links to other pages on the same Web site. If any of the links interest you, you could simply click on the link, and your Web browser would locate and load the indicated Web page. Each Web page has an address within the World Wide Web, called a **Uniform Resource Locator**, or **URL** for short. Internet Explorer displays the URL for the current page in the Address bar. For example, the URL for the Web page shown in Figure B-1 is *http://www.powells.com/*. You have already noticed a few URLs in articles you have read about the Web. Before you begin working on the Web, you are interested in knowing what the information in a URL means. After a bit of research, you discover that several components make up each URL.

▶ Each URL for a page on the World Wide Web begins with the acronym HTTP. **HTTP** (Hypertext Transfer Protocol) is the Web's communications standard. It ensures that different computers communicate in the same language when sending and receiving Web pages. This acronym is always followed by a colon and two forward slashes (*http://*) to indicate that the Web page is located on a remote Web server. A **Web server** consists of a computer or a network of computers that stores Web pages and makes them available on the Web.

▶ The name of a Web site often begins with the letters *www* (for example, *www.powells.com*), signifying that the location is part of the World Wide Web. The remainder of the site name (for example, *powells.com*) is called the **domain name**.

▶ The first component of the domain name (for example, *powells*) usually stands for the name of the institution that owns the site.

▶ The final letters are the **top-level domain** (for example, *.com*). Also known as a **global domain** or **extension**, this part of a URL suggests the kind of site or institution with which you are dealing or the country where the site or institution is located. In this case, *.com* indicates that this site is a commercial one. Table B-1 briefly describes the most common established extensions, selected country extensions, as well as new extensions being introduced. ICANN, the nonprofit corporation responsible for making Internet domain names available, is working to roll out these new top-level domains. Each top-level domain is suggested for use by a specific type of organization; however, with few exceptions any group may register a domain name using any extension.

Graphical links

Links to other Web pages can appear as graphics as well as text. Just as with text links, you can click a linked graphic to open a new Web page. Different parts of a single graphic can also contain links to separate pages. For example, a Web page might display a picture of the solar system, showing the sun and the nine planets. Each planet could serve as a link to a page containing information about that planet. Such a graphic containing multiple links is known as an image map. Because graphical links are easy to understand and use, many Web sites use them to simplify navigation.

FIGURE B-1: Links in Web pages

URL

Web page

Link

TABLE B-1: Examples of extensions

type	extensions	intended use
Established	.com	Commercial sites
	.edu	Educational institutions
	.gov	Government agencies, departments, and institutions
	.net	Network organizations (computer services that connect remote computers)
	.org	Not-for-profit organizations
Country	.cn	China
	.mx	Mexico
	.uk	United Kingdom
New	.biz	Businesses
	.info	Information service providers
	.name	For registration by individuals
	.pro	Accountants, lawyers, and physicians

Internet

Internet

Entering a URL

Most navigation on the Web is done by following links, because they make opening a Web page as simple as pointing and clicking. However, sometimes you may want to view a Web page you have heard about, but you don't have a link to the page. In this case, you need to type the page's URL. In Internet Explorer, you enter a URL in the Address text box on the Address bar. A friend gave you a list of URLs for Web sites that list volunteer and job opportunities with non-profit organizations (shown in Table B-2). Open one of the sites by typing its URL.

1. **Start Internet Explorer, then make sure the window is maximized**

2. **Click the Address text box on the Address bar**
The current URL becomes highlighted in the Address text box.

3. **Type idealist.org in the Address text box**
The old URL and page icon disappear as you type the new URL, as shown in Figure B-2. Many Web sites no longer require the optional *www.* at the start of their URLs, making it faster and easier to type the addresses.

Trouble?

If you receive an error message while trying to open the Idealist page, check the URL you entered to verify that you've typed it correctly; you can edit the URL you entered or just enter another URL listed in Table B-2.

4. **Press [Enter]**
Internet Explorer automatically adds *http://* at the beginning of the address you typed. The status indicator becomes animated, and the Idealist Web page appears shortly, as pictured in Figure B-3.

5. **Explore the page, then click the Address text box on the Address bar**
The text box still displays the URL you entered earlier. You can use your edit keys to modify this address rather than typing an entirely new URL.

6. **Click at the end of the previous URL address in the Address text box**
A flashing insertion point (text cursor) appears at the end of the URL.

7. **Press [Backspace] as many times as necessary to erase everything after http://**
The Address text box now displays only the beginning of a URL, *http://*.

8. **Type course.com/downloads/illustrated/ie6, then press [Enter]**
The status indicator becomes animated again and, after a brief time, the document window displays the Student Online Companion for this book. The Student Online Companion (SOC) is a Web page that provides links and other information you will use as you complete the steps in this book. The URL you entered includes text after the top-level domain. This part is called the path, and specifies a Web page's location within a company's Web site. The server, domain name, and top-level domain (e.g., *course.com*) identify the computer or Web site to connect to. The path (e.g., */downloads/illustrated/ie6*) describes a Web document's location on that Web site.

CLUES TO USE

AutoComplete

When you are manually entering a URL, the AutoComplete feature displays matching URLs that you have entered before, based on the letters you type. Matching URLs appear in a shortcut menu that opens below the Address Bar. If the page you want to open is listed, you can simply click it on the list to open it, rather then typing the remainder of the address.

FIGURE B-2: Entering a URL manually

Partially typed URL

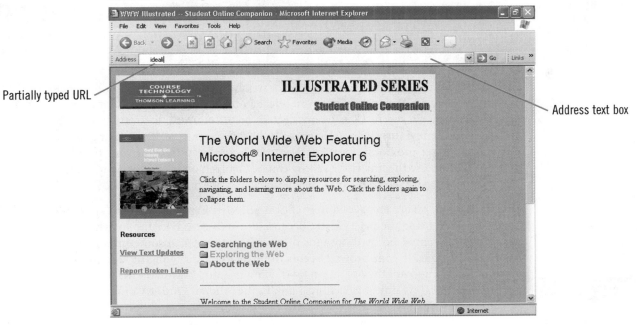

Address text box

FIGURE B-3: Home page for Idealist

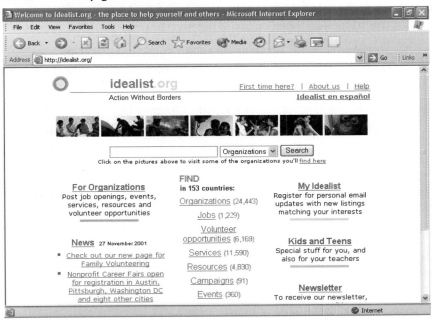

TABLE B-2: URLs of nonprofit organizations

company name	URL
Action Without Borders	idealist.org
Opportunity Nonprofit Organization Classifieds (NOCs)	opportunitynocs.org
The United Way	national.unitedway.org
Oxfam	www.oxfam.org.uk

Unit B

Internet

Finding, Starting, and Stopping Links

To make them easily recognizable, text links are always highlighted in a different color than the rest of the text on a Web page. Once you select a link, it often changes color to indicate that you have previously clicked it. Usually, unselected, or **unfollowed**, links are blue by default, while links that have previously been selected, or **followed**, are purple. By changing the color of a link, Internet Explorer provides a clear marker to help you keep track of your travels on the World Wide Web. Because the link color setting can be changed on individual computers, as well as by the creator of each Web page, links may not always appear in the default colors.

To follow a link on a Web page, simply click it. Internet Explorer will then attempt to locate and open the page, using the page's URL. Because the Web runs over the Internet, which has thousands of sites connected by thousands of networks, things can sometimes go wrong when you try to load a page. If your browser seems to be taking a very long time to locate and/or load a page, you can interrupt the operation by clicking the Stop button on the toolbar. Begin learning about using links by clicking a link in the Student Online Companion.

QuickTip

If necessary, open the Student Online Companion page by entering *course.com/downloads/illustrated/ie6* in the Address text box.

Trouble?

If you click the Stop button too soon, your document window may remain empty. Click the Refresh button to restart the loading process, then wait until the page begins to appear before clicking the Stop button.

1. In the Student Online Companion Web page, click the folder to the left of the heading **Exploring the Web**

A list of related topics appears beneath the heading.

2. Click the folder to the left of **Exploring electronic commerce**

The Web page displays a list of links to Web sites related to electronic commerce.

3. Position the mouse pointer over the **Ecommerce/Marketing Channel link**

Notice that when you move the mouse pointer over the link, its shape changes from an arrow $\aleph$ to a hand $\sqrt[h]{\ }$, as shown in Figure B-4. This transformation indicates that an image is a link.

4. Click the **Ecommerce/Marketing Channel link**; as the new Web page begins to load, click the **Stop button** on the Standard Buttons toolbar

Internet Explorer stops the process of finding and loading the linked page. When you click the Stop button, the document window displays the portion of the new page that Internet Explorer was able to load before the loading operation was halted. Internet Explorer will continue to display the current page in the document window until a new page begins loading.

5. Click the **Refresh button** on the Standard Buttons toolbar to load the page completely, then review the page contents

6. Click a link on the Ecommerce/Marketing Channel Web page

The new page opens.

FIGURE B-4: Student Online Companion page for this book

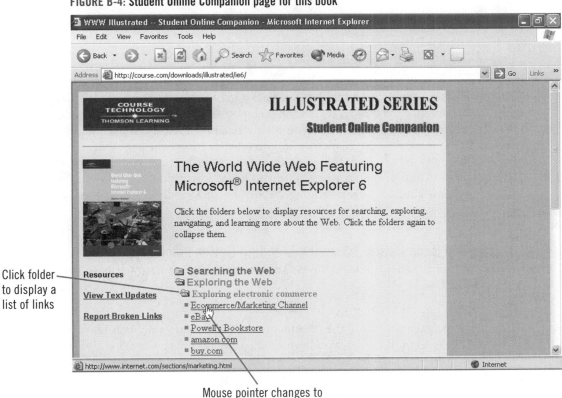

Click folder to display a list of links

Mouse pointer changes to a hand when positioned over a link

Setting a home page

Internet Explorer's default home page is set by the organization that provides the use of the browser to you. The default home page often includes advertisements that the provider wants you to view. However, you can change your home page to any page available on the Web. This enables you to open one Web page that's most useful to you by clicking the Home button. To set a Web page as your home page, first open the page in the browser, either by following a link or by entering its URL. Then click Tools on the menu bar, and click Internet Options to open the Internet Options dialog box, as shown in Figure B-5. Click the Use Current button, then click OK. Alternately, you can open the Internet Options dialog box, enter the URL for the new home page in the Address text box, then click the Use Current button. You can change your home page as often as you want; however, when working in a computer lab or on someone else's computer, you should ask the lab monitor or the computer's owner before changing the home page.

FIGURE B-5: Internet Options dialog box

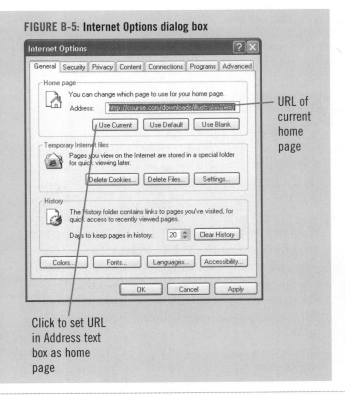

URL of current home page

Click to set URL in Address text box as home page

Internet

Moving Backward and Forward

Internet Explorer makes it easy to navigate backward and forward through Web pages you have previously viewed. As you navigate among Web pages, Internet Explorer maintains a list of the URLs you have opened, in the order you have viewed them. You can click the Back button on the toolbar to display the page you viewed immediately before the page you are currently viewing. If you have used the Back button to return to an earlier page and then want to move to a later page, you can use the Forward button to move forward in the series of pages you have viewed. Practice moving among Web pages you've recently opened using the Back and Forward buttons.

Steps

QuickTip

When the Back and Forward buttons display a list arrow to the right, you can click the arrow, then select from a list of previously visited pages. This feature lets you instantly jump to a page without clicking through the intervening pages.

1. Click the **Back button** ⬅ on the Standard Buttons toolbar once

The previously viewed page, the E-Commerce/Marketing Channel page, appears in your document window.

2. Click ⬅ until it turns gray

Your home page appears in the document window. As shown in Figure B-6, the Back button is now gray to indicate that you have reached the first page viewed and that this button is temporarily unavailable for use. The figures in this book show the Student Online Companion page as the home page; your home page might be different.

3. Click the **Forward button** ➡ on the Standard Buttons toolbar three times

The Ecommerce/Marketing Channel page appears, as shown in Figure B-7. Notice that both the Back and Forward buttons are now active (not gray).

4. Click ⬅ until you return to the Student Online Companion page

CLUES TO USE

Problems when moving between pages

Occasionally you will navigate to Web sites where the Back and Forward buttons don't seem to work properly. This can result from a site's use of technologies that direct you to a Web page designed for people from your country or who speak your preferred language. When you click a link to such a site, the target page opens only for a fraction of a second, evaluates your location and/or language preferences, and then opens another Web page based on that information. If you then click the Back button, you open the evaluation page, which simply re-evaluates your settings and returns you to the page you just left. To escape this cycle and move back in the navigation history,

click the arrow on the Back button, then click the title of the page to which you want to return.

Another situation you may encounter while navigating the Web is the opening of an additional browser window. This may happen when you click a link and your target page opens in a new window, or when you go to a particular Web site and an advertisement associated with the site opens in a new window. In both cases, the Back button is not functional because there are no earlier pages to return to in the new browser window. Simply close the new browser window that opened when you're finished looking at the Web page.

FIGURE B-6: Student Online Companion page

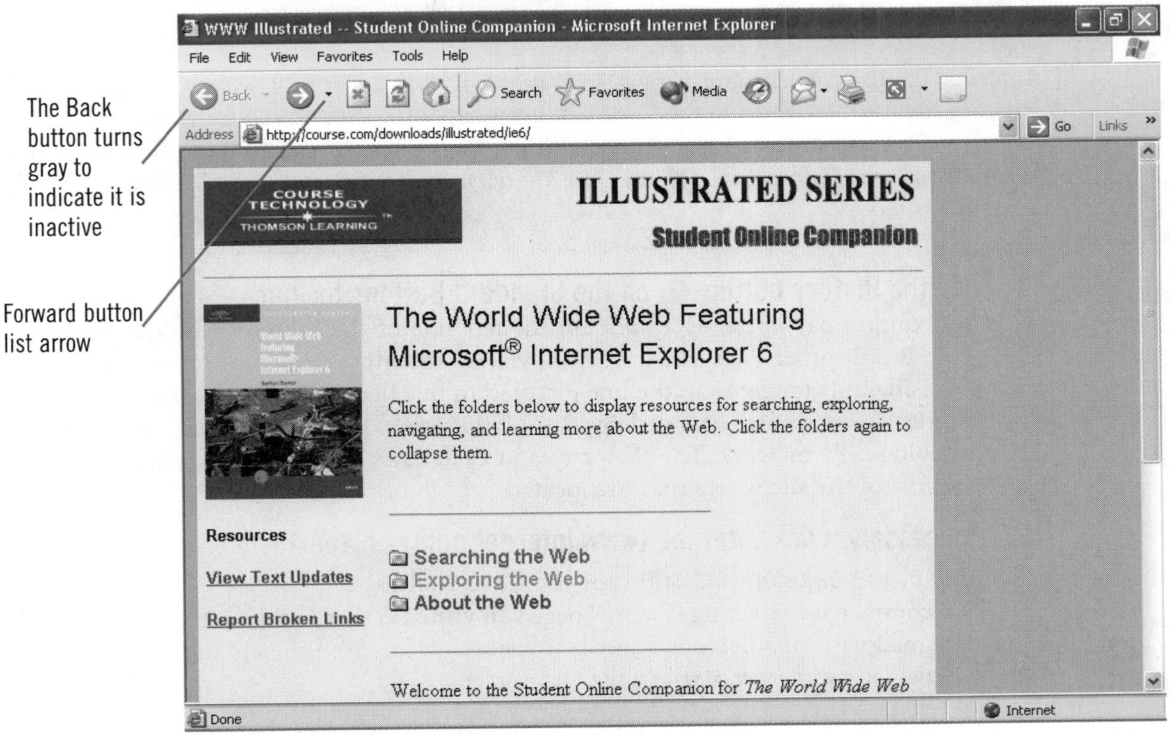

The Back button turns gray to indicate it is inactive

Forward button list arrow

FIGURE B-7: The Ecommerce/Marketing Channel page

The Back and Forward buttons are both active

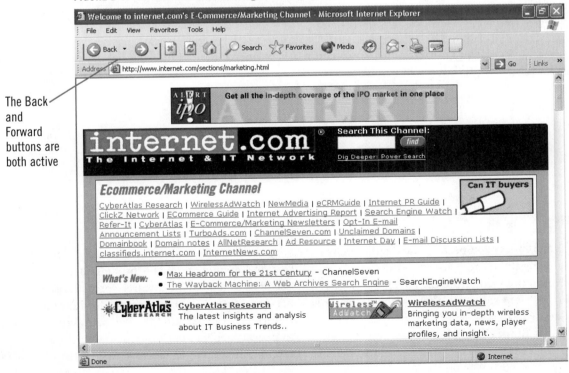

Internet

Viewing History

Internet Explorer offers another way to move among previously selected Web pages—the History list. Instead of using the Back and Forward buttons to search for a previously viewed page, you can go straight to that page by clicking the History button and then selecting its name from the History list. ✎ Use the History list to review the Web pages you have already visited.

Trouble?

If your History list is not grouped by days of the week like the one in Figure B-8, click the list arrow to the right of the word "View" at the top of the Explorer bar, then click By Date on the menu.

1. Click the **History button** ⊚ on the Standard Buttons toolbar

The Explorer bar opens as a pane on the left side of the browser window, as shown in Figure B-8. If other Web sites have been viewed recently with your browser, your list may be considerably longer than the one pictured in this figure. By default, the sites shown for the selected week are arranged by day of the week, and sites visited earlier are listed chronologically by week. The Web pages in each day's list are arranged alphabetically by the name of the site where they are located.

2. If necessary, click **internet (www.internet.com)** on the History list to display the name of the page on this site that you have visited

The Ecommerce/Marketing Channel page you visited earlier in the unit is located on a Web site named *www.internet.com*. Pages you viewed on this Web site are therefore listed under "internet (*www.internet.com*)" in the History list.

3. Click **Welcome to internet.com's E-Commerce/Marketing Channel** under the internet (www.internet.com) heading in the History list

The page you viewed earlier reopens in the Web page window.

QuickTip

Click the Search button 🔍 next to the View menu on the Explorer bar to replace the History list with a generic form that allows you to search for information on the Web.

4. Click the list arrow to the right of the word "View" at the top of the Explorer bar

The Explorer bar View menu opens, as shown in Figure B-9. This menu offers different options for organizing the display of history information.

5. Click ⊚

The History frame closes and the Ecommerce/Marketing Channel page appears across the entire browser window.

What is the Explorer bar?

The Explorer bar lets you perform activities, such as navigating using the History list or searching for information on the Web, while the current Web page appears on the right side of the browser window. This format allows you to select and view pages from the Explorer bar without closing it. For example, if you click the Search button on the Standard Buttons toolbar, the Explorer bar opens on the left side of the browser window and displays a form for searching on the Web, while continuing to show the site you are currently viewing in the right frame of the browser window. You can use the form to search for information and then open one of the suggested Web sites. In addition to displaying a search form and the History list, you can use the Explorer bar to show your Favorites list by clicking the Favorites button on the toolbar. When you click the Media button on the toolbar, the Explorer bar provides controls for playing media files. Lastly, you can navigate through files and folders on your computer and network with the Explorer bar by clicking View on the menu bar, pointing to Explorer Bar, then clicking Folders.

FIGURE B-8: **History list**

Explorer bar

View list arrow

History list organized chronologically

Each day's entries organized alphabetically by Web server

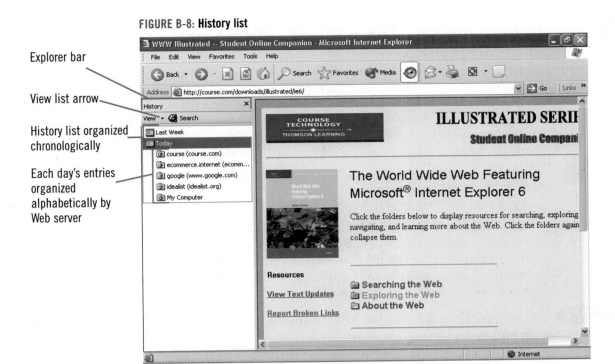

FIGURE B-9: **Explorer bar View menu**

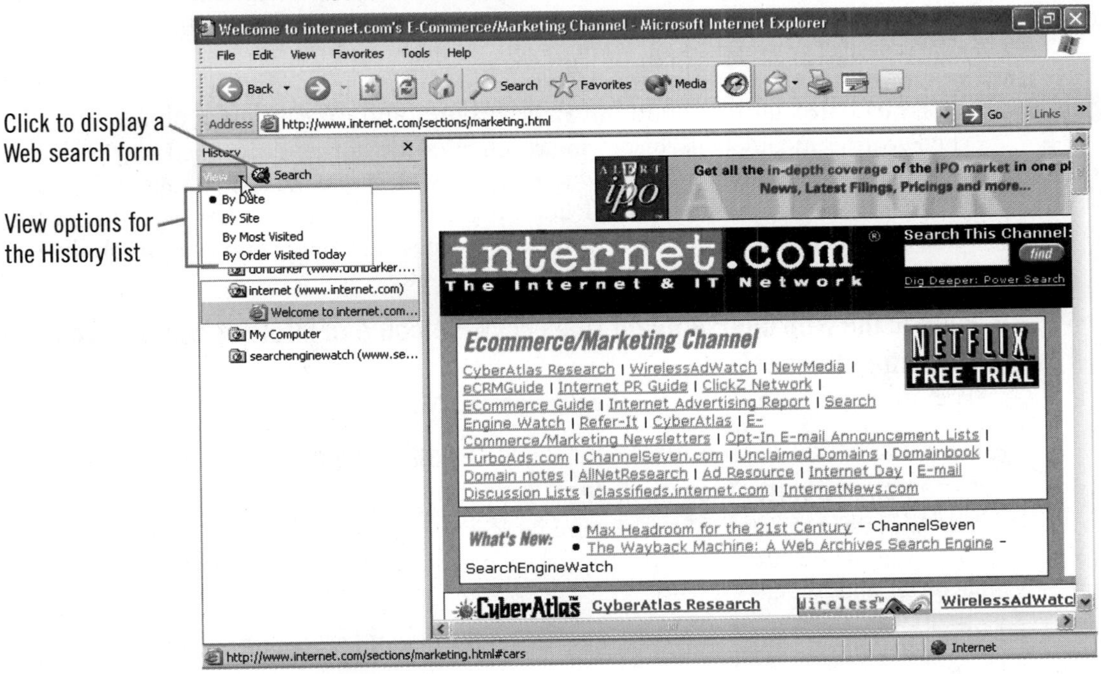

Click to display a Web search form

View options for the History list

Internet

Using Favorites

Internet Explorer provides a convenient feature called the Favorites menu that lets you collect and organize links to the Web pages that are the most useful and interesting to you. You can add Web page links to your Favorites menu and organize the links/URLs into folders by subject. The Favorites menu provides another tool for returning to Web pages that you have already visited. Favorites are especially useful for pages that you find particularly significant and expect to visit repeatedly. ◢▬▬ Practice creating and organizing favorites by adding one for the current Web page.

1. **Make sure the Ecommerce/Marketing Channel page appears in your document window, click Favorites on the menu bar, then click Add to Favorites**
   The Add Favorite dialog box opens. The Name text box shows the text that will be used to identify this Web page on the Favorites list; the page title that appears in the browser's title bar is used as the default. Although you can edit the Web page name, you decide that the default name is a good description of the page.

QuickTip

To create a button for a favorite on the Links toolbar, create a favorite in the Links folder on the Favorites menu.

2. **If your Add Favorite window does not display the New Folder button, click the Create in button**
   The Add Favorite dialog box expands to include options for placing the new favorite within a folder on the Favorites menu as shown in Figure B-10. Creating and using folders helps keep your favorites organized and makes it easier to find them in the Favorites menu.

3. **Click the New Folder button, type Web course in the Folder name text box, then click OK**
   The Create New Folder dialog box closes, and you return to the Add Favorite dialog box, with the new folder highlighted on the Favorites list.

4. **Click OK to add this page to the selected folder in your Favorites list with the default name, then click the Home button 🏠 on the Standard Buttons toolbar**
   Your home page appears in the document window.

QuickTip

Click the Favorites button on the Standard Buttons toolbar to display your Favorites list in the Explorer bar.

5. **Click Favorites on the menu bar (not on the Standard Buttons toolbar)**
   The Favorites menu opens, displaying commands for working with the Favorites list as well as the favorites themselves, as shown in Figure B-11. Notice that the Links and Media folders appear beneath these options, in addition to the Web course folder that you created. The Links and Media folders contain pre-set favorites that open information about Internet Explorer, as well as other Microsoft-owned Web sites.

6. **Point to the Web course folder, then click Welcome to internet.com's E-Commerce/Marketing Channel**
   The Favorites menu closes and the Ecommerce/Marketing Channel page opens.

7. **Click Favorites on the menu bar, click Organize Favorites, click the Web course folder, click Delete, then click Yes**
   The favorite and folder you added are removed from the list. If your Favorites list becomes too large or you find that some favorites are no longer valid or useful, you can remove favorites and folders.

8. **Click Close in the Organize Favorites dialog box, then click 🏠**

FIGURE B-10: **Add Favorite dialog box**

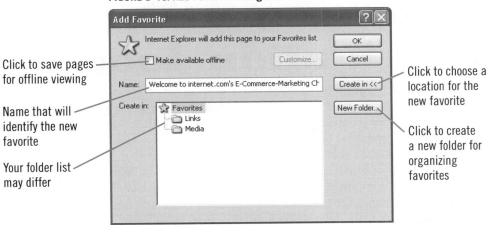

Click to save pages for offline viewing

Name that will identify the new favorite

Your folder list may differ

Click to choose a location for the new favorite

Click to create a new folder for organizing favorites

FIGURE B-11: **Favorites menu**

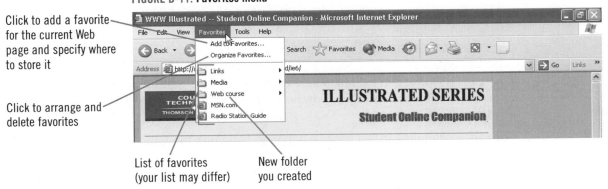

Click to add a favorite for the current Web page and specify where to store it

Click to arrange and delete favorites

List of favorites (your list may differ)

New folder you created

CLUES TO USE

Viewing Web pages offline

Internet Explorer allows you to view selected pages from your Favorites list even when you are offline, or not connected to the Web. You mark pages on your Favorites list that you want to view offline, and then Internet Explorer saves copies of the Web page files for these marked pages, along with any associated image files, to your computer. You can then view these pages on any browser, whether or not you are connected to the Internet. Viewing pages offline allows you to save pages you haven't thoroughly read and view them later when you don't have access to the Web (for example, when using a laptop on an airplane).

To mark a page to be available offline, click the Make available offline check box in the Add Favorite dialog box. You can also click an existing favorite in the Organize Favorites dialog box, then click the Make available offline check box. You can use the Customize button in the Add Favorite dialog box or the Properties button in the Organize Favorites dialog box to set how often you would like the page updated on your hard drive and to specify whether you want pages linked to from the current page to be saved offline as well. After you mark all the pages you want to view offline, click Tools, then click Synchronize to download and save an up-to-date version of each marked page. Click File on the menu bar, then click Work Offline to let Internet Explorer know that you want to use saved pages while browsing rather than download new versions from the Web.

Working with Navigation Tools

Internet Explorer includes many tools for moving between Web pages (the Back, Forward, and Home buttons) and around an individual Web page (the scroll bar). In addition, many pages on the Web that are grouped together into Web sites offer their own navigation features. The most common, a **navigation bar**, is a set of links running down the left or right side, or across the top, of a Web page. Web sites for large organizations or those that include a lot of information may be composed of hundreds or even thousands of separate Web pages. However, well-designed Web sites include consistent navigation tools on every page, helping you to keep track of where you are within the Web site, and allowing you to efficiently find the information you're looking for. ✒ Practice recognizing and using navigation tools by opening a Web site that incorporates a navigation bar.

1. Click in the **Address text box**, enter the URL **course.com**, then press **[Enter]**
   Your document window displays the Course Technology home page, as shown in Figure B-12. The page includes three separate navigation bars: two across the top and one down the left edge. In general, the links in navigation bars at the top of a page take you to different sections of a Web site, while a navigation bar down the side offers options related to the current page's content.

Trouble?

If you don't see this link or the link for a subsequent step in your browser, click any link in the same navigation bar.

2. Click the **Internet** link on the navigation bar that runs down the side of the page
   A new Web page from the Course Technology Web site opens in your browser, as shown in Figure B-13. Notice that the links along the left side of the page offer the same topic choices as on the site's home page. The navigation bars along the top of the page remain consistent as well.

3. Click the **Series** link in the upper navigation bar along the top of the page
   Another Web page from the Course Technology site opens. By clicking a link at the top of the page, you moved to a different section of the site. The navigation bar along the left side of the page changed to provide options relevant to this section of the site. However, the two navigation bars at the top of the page are identical to those in previous Web pages from *course.com*, providing a consistent and predictable way to move between the site's sections.

4. Click **Continuing education** in the navigation bar on the left side of the page
   The Continuing Education page opens, replacing the left navigation bar with a new set of options.

5. Click **Home** in the top navigation bar to return to the course.com home page

6. Exit Internet Explorer

Working with frames

Some Web page authors add navigation bars to Web sites using a special design tool known as frames. The frames feature changes the way your browser displays the Web page, dividing the Internet Explorer document window into multiple windows. Each of these windows displays a separate Web document. Thus, a designer could split the window into a narrow band along the left side, which displays the navigation bar, and the rest of the window, which displays the page content. Using frames has some advantages, including slightly quicker download times and the ability to scroll one section of the page while leaving the other in place. Frames come with some disadvantages for Web page authors, though—for example, not all browsers display frames consistently. As a result, many sites have eliminated frames from their Web pages. If you see more than one horizontal scroll bar in the browser window, however, the page you're viewing uses frames.

FIGURE B-12: Navigation bars on Course Technology home page

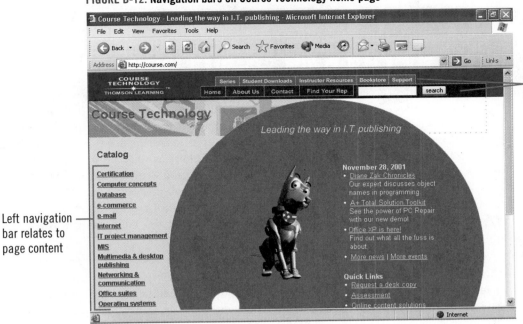

Two top navigation bars open different sections of site

Left navigation bar relates to page content

FIGURE B-13: New Web page maintains Web site navigation structure

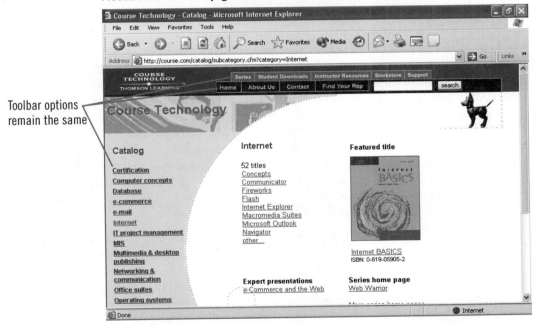

Toolbar options remain the same

Internet

Understanding Security Issues

Using the Web offers access to a huge collection of information and tools. However, Web browsing is not without dangers, generally known as **security risks**. These risks include the possible interception of information you provide online, threats to the safety of your computer, and potential breaches of your anonymity. While security risks are manageable and can be minimized, it's important to understand potential pitfalls and to have a plan for avoiding them every time you use the Web. Through a combination of tailoring browser settings and interacting knowledgably with requests from Web sites you use, you can take advantage of the Web's many resources while protecting your computer and keeping information about yourself private. Review the three main types of security risks on the Web, along with options for addressing them.

Details

▶ **Data Confidentiality:** Many Web users take advantage of the Web's convenience to order goods or services online. Such transactions generally require the purchaser to provide sensitive financial information, such as a credit card number, expiration date, and billing address. Just like protecting receipts when you use a credit card in person, it's important to ensure that this information stays confidential, in order to prevent a third party from using your credit card fraudulently. In practice, almost all sites that request such financial information on the Web do it securely, but you should always verify that you're using a secure Web page before providing this information on a new or unfamiliar Web site. Internet Explorer provides two ways to check a Web page's security. First, the URL for a secure Web page always begins with *https* instead of *http*. The *s* stands for "secure." Second, when Internet Explorer opens a secure Web page, it displays 🔒 in the status bar, near the right edge of the window. When a page asks for sensitive information and displays both of these security hallmarks, you can be confident that the data will not be intercepted between your computer and its destination.

▶ **Computer Safety:** In addition to including basic elements like text and graphics, Web pages can include programs. Known as **scripts**, **controls**, or **applets**, most of these programs simply enable Web pages to interact with users—for instance, a script enables the clickable folder structure on the Student Online Companion for this book. However, a Web site can also include malicious programs, which can cause problems as minor as forcing Internet Explorer to close or as major as deleting the contents of a user's hard drive. To address these risks, Internet Explorer blocks programs from running when they are likely to be malicious. You can view Internet Explorer's security settings by clicking Tools on the menu bar, clicking Internet Options, then clicking the Security tab. Internet Explorer categorizes Web pages into four zones. To view the security settings for pages on the Internet, click the Internet icon, then click Custom Level to open the Security Settings dialog box, as shown in Figure B-14. When you're finished viewing the settings, click the Cancel button to avoid changing any settings.

▶ **Personal Anonymity:** As you browse the Web, many Web sites attempt to store small text files on your computer. Known as **cookies**, these files can contain information about when you visited a site and which pages you viewed, along with any information you may have provided the site during your visit, such as the country in which you live and the language in which you prefer to read pages. Cookies are a contentious issue between companies that own Web sites and people who use them. While some cookies are stored on your machine merely to allow the site to provide you customized content whenever you return, other cookies can be used to collect data about your Internet use for marketing purposes. As with malicious programs, Internet Explorer blocks certain cookies by default and enables you to edit settings to fit your Web usage requirements. To view settings for cookies, open the Internet Options dialog box by clicking Tools on the menu bar, clicking Internet Options, then clicking the Privacy tab, as shown in Figure B-15. You can use the slider to select from several pre-set cookie-handling options.

FIGURE B-14: Security Settings dialog box

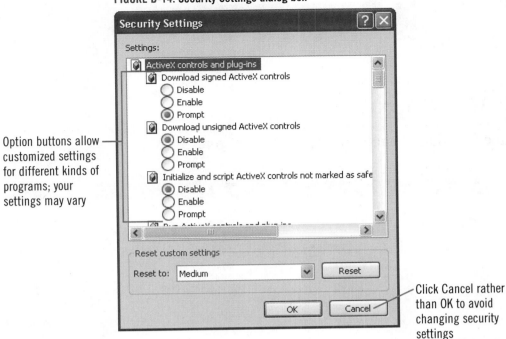

Option buttons allow customized settings for different kinds of programs; your settings may vary

Click Cancel rather than OK to avoid changing security settings

FIGURE B-15: Privacy tab in the Internet Options dialog box

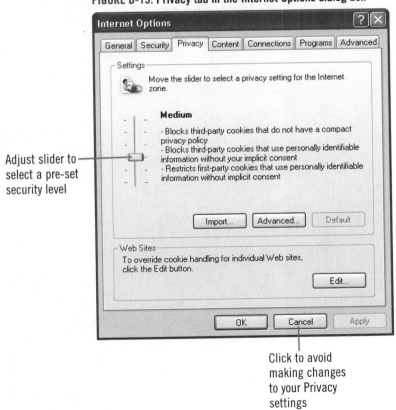

Adjust slider to select a pre-set security level

Click to avoid making changes to your Privacy settings

Internet

Practice

▶ Concepts Review

Describe the function of each button shown in Figure B-16.

FIGURE B-16

Match each term below with its definition.

7. **Links**	**a.** A set of links running down the left or right side of a Web page, or across the top
8. **URL**	**b.** Web page address
9. **Explorer bar**	**c.** Web page elements that you can click to open other Web pages
10. **Navigation bar**	**d.** Small text files stored on your computer by Web sites you visit
11. **Cookies**	**e.** Window displaying tools such as the History list, Favorites, or Search form

Select the best answer from the list of choices.

12. To view the previous page:
   a. Click the Previous command on the Go menu.
   b. Select the Backup command on the Go menu.
   c. Click the Previous button.
   d. Click the Back button.

13. The Favorites menu lets you do everything *except*:
   a. Store a link to the current page in a folder.
   b. Open the Organize Favorites dialog box.
   c. Move a page around the Web.
   d. Add the current page to the Favorites list.

14. The History list lets you do everything *except*:
   a. Create a new link.
   b. View the History list by page title.
   c. Search for a particular previously viewed page.
   d. View a previously visited page.

15. Which URL is incorrect?
   a. http://www.company.com/home.html
   b. http://www.company/home.html
   c. http://www.company.com
   d. http://www.company.com/homepage.html

16. HTTP stands for:
   a. Hypertext Translate Protocol.
   b. Hypertext Transfer Pilot.
   c. Hypertext Transport Pointer.
   d. Hypertext Transfer Protocol.

17. The _____ usually follows *www.* in a Web site's name and tells you both the name of the Web site and the type of institution it is.
   a. Top-level domain
   b. Origin name
   c. URL
   d. Domain name

Internet

18. The global domain *.org* **suggests the Web site you are accessing is a(n):**
  a. Commercial site.
  b. Military site.
  c. Nonprofit organization site.
  d. Educational site.

19. To protect your anonymity on the Web, you should:
  a. Verify that a Web page is secure before sending sensitive data.
  b. Check settings on the Security tab of the Internet Options dialog box.
  c. Check settings in the Security Settings dialog box.
  d. Check cookie settings on the Privacy tab of the Internet Options dialog box.

20. To protect the confidentiality of your data on the Web, you should:
  a. Verify that a Web page is secure before sending sensitive data.
  b. Check settings on the Security tab of the Internet Options dialog box.
  c. Check settings in the Security Settings dialog box.
  d. Check cookie settings on the Privacy tab of the Internet Options dialog box.

21. Which is another term for a link?
  a. URL
  b. Top-level domain
  c. Hyperlink
  d. Frame

 Skills Review

1. Enter a URL.
  a. Start Internet Explorer.
  b. Click the Address text box on the Address bar.
  c. In the Location text box, type **www.ibm.com**, then Press [Enter].
  d. Explore this Web site, using the techniques and tools you learned about in this unit.
  e. Click the Home button on the Standard Buttons toolbar when you have finished, then exit Internet Explorer.

2. Find, start, and stop links.
  a. Start Internet Explorer.
  b. Click in the Address text box, type **www.course.com/downloads/illustrated/ie6**, then press [Enter].
  c. On the Student Online Companion page, click the Exploring the Web folder, then click the Exploring employment folder.
  d. Click one of the links in the list that appears, then click the Stop button on the toolbar before the page finishes loading.
  e. Click the Refresh button to finish loading the page.
  f. On the employment page you opened, click a link to open another Web page.

3. Move backward and forward.
a. Click the Back button to return to the employment page you opened.

b. Click the Forward button to see the related page you opened.

c. Continue to click the Back button until it turns gray.

d. Click a link on the current page. Once the new page loads, click a link on that page.

e. Use the Back and Forward buttons to locate the Student Online Companion page.

4. View History.
a. Click the History button on the Standard Buttons toolbar.

b. Click the name of the site containing the employment page you opened above, then click the link for the employment page.

c. Click the Home button.

d. Use the Back button list arrow to return to the employment page you just viewed.

e. Close the Explorer bar.

5. Use Favorites.
a. Click in the Address text box, type **www.course.com/downloads/illustrated/ie6**, then press [Enter].

b. Click the Add to Favorites command on the Favorites menu, if necessary click Create in, click New Folder, type **Internet Explorer**, then click OK twice.

c. On the Student Online Companion, click the Exploring the Web folder, click the Exploring Web media folder, then click one of the links on the list that appears.

d. Use the Favorites menu to return to the WWW Illustrated—Student Online Companion page.

e. If you're working in a computer lab, remove the Favorite and the folder you added.

6. Work with navigation tools.
a. Click in the Address text box, type **microsoft.com**, then press [Enter].

b. Examine the home page to identify the number of navigation bars present and to get a sense of the function of each within the Web site.

c. Click a link on the left navigation bar.

d. Examine the navigation bars present on the new page that opened.

e. Click a link on a navigation bar along the top of the page.

f. Click the Home button on the Standard Buttons toolbar to display your home page.

g. Exit Internet Explorer.

Independent Challenge 1

You are the administrative assistant to Natalie Hernandez, the president of Talk It Up, a small promotional company that specializes in creating print ads and promotional pieces. Natalie wants to upgrade the office scanner to enhance the quality of the graphics included in the company's offerings. Natalie has narrowed the search to three manufacturers, and she asks you to investigate their offerings using the Web. The manufacturers' URLs are:

    www.canon.com
    www.lexmark.com
    epson.com

Use Internet Explorer to research the information available on the Web for each firm's scanners, then print a page from the site of the firm you think offers the most appealing high-end scanners. Be sure to write your name on the page after you print it.

 # Independent Challenge 2

You recently landed a job as a columnist for a popular computer magazine. One of your responsibilities will be to write a monthly column called "Tech Notes," which will chronicle the latest developments in software technology. Add the following Web sites to a new folder on your Favorites list so you can browse them for information that will help you stay abreast of the activities of the major players in the computer software industry:

    microsoft.com
    www.adobe.com
    apple.com
    redhat.com

Once you store the initial pages of these sites in the Favorites list, use the list to revisit the initial page for each site and investigate the company's offerings. Print a page of the site that most impresses you, and then remove the folder containing the favorites you added from the Favorites list.

Independent Challenge 3

In a few months, you will graduate from college with a teaching degree. You have been investigating the job market, but you are also interested in traveling and perhaps teaching in a different country. A friend suggests that you consider the Peace Corps, and you decide to look into the organization. Use the URL www.peacecorps.gov to research the Peace Corps.

Explore the site, then print a page containing useful information. Be sure to write your name on the page after you print it.

Independent Challenge 4

You are teaching a course on British government. You're preparing to assign a research project to your students to discuss and compare the main bodies of British government—the Cabinet, the House of Commons, and the House of Lords. You want to require your students to do some of their research on the Internet. You investigate a list of URLs for British government sites given to you by a colleague, to make sure this is a reasonable expectation. To complete this Independent Challenge, open and investigate the offerings on the following Web sites. Keep written notes on each site, recording the types of information available and the approximate number of Web pages for each. After you have surveyed each site, use a word-processing program to write a paragraph discussing whether or not you think the Internet is a reasonable source of information for this project. Be sure to type your name on the document before printing.

www.number-10.gov.uk
www.parliament.uk

► Visual Workshop

Use the skills you learned in this lesson to open the Web page shown below, then navigate as necessary to activate both the Back and Forward buttons, as shown in Figure B-17. Print a copy of the page. Note that because most Web sites are updated on a regular basis, the content and/or layout of the Web page that you print may differ from the content and layout of the page shown in Figure B-17.

FIGURE B-17

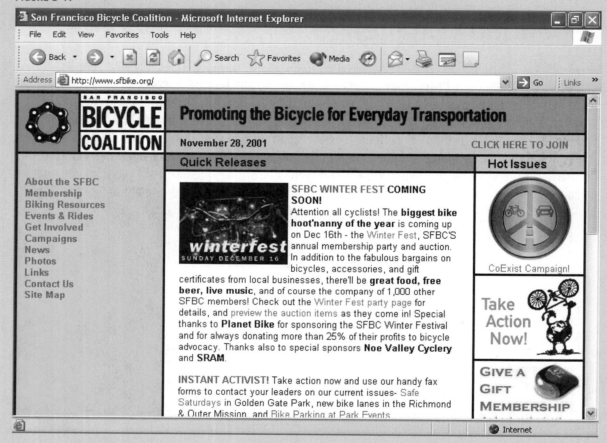

Searching
the Web

Objectives

- ► **Understand search methods**
- ► **Search by subject**
- ► **Search by content**
- ► **Metasearch by content**
- ► **Search by collection**
- ► **Search for a location**
- ► **Search for a person**
- ► **Search for merchandise**

The World Wide Web is an enormous network, and when you want to find information on a particular topic, simply navigating from one page to the next is a very slow and inefficient way to go about it. Fortunately, a number of search tools available on the Web can help you quickly locate what you want. Using these tools, you can find information about a specific subject, a particular geographical location, or an acquaintance whose address information you need. ✐ In this unit, you will learn how to use search tools effectively and efficiently to locate information.

Understanding Search Methods

Information on the Web grows rapidly, is not well organized, and sometimes proves inaccurate. As a consequence, it is important to search as effectively and efficiently as possible. Some search tools are better for finding a specific type of information than others. Typically, an integrated approach that combines the available search tools gives you the best chance of finding the information you want. Table C-1 lists strategies for finding information with each of the major search tools that will be discussed in this unit. ✐ To use your time most effectively when doing Web research, use the following integrated strategies, or guidelines, to minimize your search time and maximize search results:

Details

▶ Search broadly at first to determine the breadth of information available on the subject.

▶ Search narrowly and deeply to find specific information.

▶ Search multiple sources simultaneously to ensure greater coverage of the Web.

▶ Look for pages with collections of links about a subject.

▶ Use map sites to find location information and directions.

▶ Use people finder sites to find contact information for people or organizations.

▶ Use product indices to locate online stores selling particular merchandise and to compare prices.

TABLE C-1: Strategies for searching the Web

to find	example information	search by/for	tool	example tools
General categories of information	Computers and Internet	Subject	**Subject directories** are hand-compiled lists of sites grouped and arranged by topic	Yahoo! and Galaxy
Narrow and specific information	Advantages of a flat-panel computer monitor	Content	**Search engines** automatically scan the Web and index it by keyword	Google
Extensive resources for narrow and specific information	Advantages of a flat-panel computer monitor	Content	**Metasearch engines** offer single forms for querying multiple search engines' indices simultaneously	Dogpile and Metacrawler
Pages with collections of links about a subject	Information about search engines	Collection	**Collections** are guide pages with useful information about a subject	Search Engine Watch and Browser Watch
Location information and directions	25 Thomson Place, Boston, Massachusetts, USA	Location	**Map sites** create maps showing the location of an address you enter	Mapquest and Yahoo! Maps
A person's phone, address, or e-mail	A lost business contact	People	**People finders** are searchable indices for locating people	Switchboard and 411 Locate
Online stores selling a particular product	Flat-panel computer monitor vendors	Merchandise	**Product indices** list prices from many vendors for comparison shopping	CNET shopping and Ebay

Additional search tools

Internet Explorer 6 offers several features to help with searches, such as AutoSearch, Related Links, and the Media Bar. AutoSearch lets you type a search query directly into the Address Bar of your browser and uses the Microsoft search engine to locate possible matches on the Web. Related Links is an optional feature on the Tools menu that provides you with a list of sites similar to the one you are currently viewing in your browser. The Media Bar helps you find audio and video you can access over the Web. For details about these search features, visit the Microsoft Web site at *http://www.microsoft.com/windows/ie.*

Internet

Internet

Searching by Subject

If you are not sure where to start investigating a subject or if you want to obtain a quick overview of a subject, begin your search with a subject directory. A **subject directory** is a list of links to general information topics, arranged alphabetically to facilitate browsing. Experts usually compile subject directories, making them fairly reliable search tools. These hand-compiled directories typically list subtopics beneath each major heading, as shown in Figure C-1. The hierarchical organization, or hierarchical tree, in a subject directory lets you quickly browse through the available subjects and their subtopics. ◢━━━ As you begin using the Internet, you regularly run across unfamiliar technical terms. Use the Yahoo! subject directory to identify technical dictionaries available on the Web.

1. Open Internet Explorer, type **www.course.com/downloads/illustrated/ie6** in the Address text box on the Address bar, then press **[Enter]**
   The Student Online Companion for this book opens in the document window.

2. Click the **Searching the Web folder**, then click the **Searching by subject folder**
   A list of links to subject directories appears below the Searching by subject folder.

Trouble?

If you are unable to connect to Yahoo! (for example, you receive an error message or the page fails to load after a long time), click the link for another subject directory instead.

3. Click **Yahoo!**
   The Yahoo! page opens, as shown in Figure C-2. The top of the page features a Search box to assist in locating a subject. (You will learn about search boxes and forms in the "Searching by Content" lesson.) For now, you will browse the subject directory just below the Search box to gain an overview of the business resources available on the Web.

4. Click **Computers & Internet** in the subject directory, then scroll down the page that loads to view the options available on the subject list
   A list of topics having to do with computers and the Internet appears, as shown in Figure C-3.

5. Click **Dictionaries**
   A directory of online dictionaries appears.

6. Scroll down the list and examine the descriptions of available resources

QuickTip

To return to the Student Online Companion, use the Back button, the History list, or enter the following URL in the Address text box: *www.course.com/downloads/ illustrated/ie6.*

7. When you have finished, return to the Student Online Companion

FIGURE C-1: Alphabetical and hierarchical structure of a subject directory

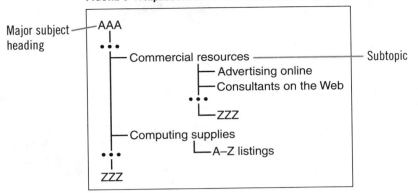

Major subject heading → AAA

•••

— Commercial resources ——————— Subtopic
— Advertising online
— Consultants on the Web

•••

└ ZZZ

— Computing supplies
└ A–Z listings

•••

ZZZ

FIGURE C-2: Yahoo! home page

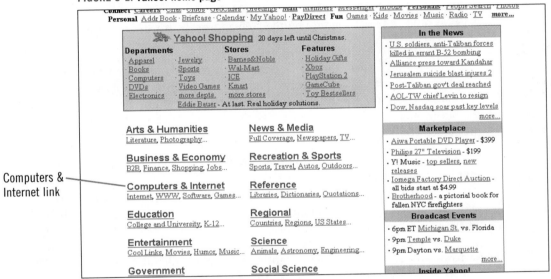

Computers & Internet link

FIGURE C-3: Listing of computers & Internet subtopics on Yahoo!

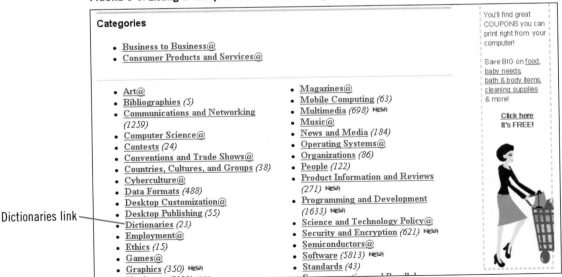

Dictionaries link

Internet

Searching by Content

When you want to find specific information, your best option is a search engine. A **search engine** lets you specify keywords or phrases in order to retrieve a list of links to pages on the Web that contain matching information. A search engine uses a special program called a **spider** to travel from one Web site to another, indexing the contents of the Web pages at each site. The **index** created by the spider is simply a list of the keywords with links to the pages on which they appear. To search an index, you enter a query using keywords and phrases in a search form provided by the search engine. A more precisely worded query will yield more relevant results.

You've seen computers using flat panel monitors in stores and computer labs, and you're curious about the advantages this type of monitor offers. Use a search engine to find information about this specific topic.

Steps

1. On the Student Online Companion, click the **Searching the Web folder**, then click the **Searching by content folder**

A list of links to search engines on the Web appears below the Searching by content folder.

Trouble?

If Google is unavailable, click the link for another search engine instead.

2. Click **Google**

The simple search form for the Google search engine opens, as shown in Figure C-4. All search engines provide you with two basic elements to use to search. The **Search text box** is where you enter the word or words for which you want to search. The **Search button** is the button that you click in order to start the search once you have entered information in the Search text box.

3. Click in the **Search text box** to make the insertion point appear, then type **"flat panel monitor" advantages**

The search statement must contain double quotes (" ") around "flat panel monitor." This format tells the Google search engine to look only for pages that contain these three words together in the precise order in which you have entered them (i.e., when they appear as a phrase) and that also contain the word "advantages." The ability to search for an exact phrase narrows your search results significantly. If you don't add quotes or otherwise indicate that you are searching for an exact phrase, the search engine will match every page indexed that contains all of the keywords, regardless of where they appear in the pages. This can make the search much less useful for finding relevant information.

4. Click the **Search button**

The search page reloads, showing the results of the query. If the AutoComplete dialog box opens, click No to close it.

QuickTip

Search results may also contain other useful hints, such as relevancy scores. These scores rate and arrange retrieved Web pages according to how closely they match your query. Relevancy scoring typically uses the proximity of keywords (that is, how close the words are to one another) on a page and their frequency on a page to rank the results of a search.

5. Scroll down the page to see the results

The results appear below the search form, beginning with a summary statement that specifies the number of pages matching your query, as shown in Figure C-5. Google displays the results sorted according to how closely they match your query. Highlighted links may also appear at the top and along the right side. These links, known as **sponsored links**, are valid matches to your query, but they are given prominence on the results page because an advertiser has paid Google to feature them.

6. Click the first, most relevant link

A page appears in your document window.

7. Examine the page, then return to the results page

8. Scroll to the bottom of the page, then click **Next**

The page containing the next set of links leading to matching pages appears.

9. When you have finished, return to the Student Online Companion

FIGURE C-4: Google search form

Enter words or phrases to search for here

Click to view a list of matches from Google's database

Click to open the Web page that matches your request most closely

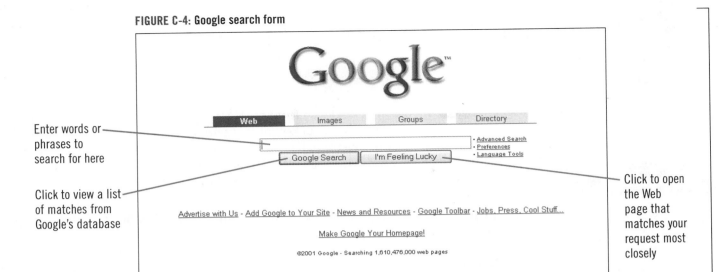

FIGURE C-5: Google search results

Estimated number of Web pages found by search

Links to advertisers who paid for their sites to be featured

Links to matching documents

Constructing successful queries

You can improve the relevance of results from a search engine by constructing your queries using Boolean operators. **Boolean operators** are special connecting words that indicate the relationship among the keywords in your search statement. The term Boolean refers to George Boole, who pioneered the branch of mathematics that uses these operators.

The Boolean operators AND, OR, and NOT let you narrow, broaden, or exclude information retrieved in a search, respectively. Search engines vary in their level and support of Boolean operators, so you should read the Help section of the particular search engine with which you are working for tips on using the available Boolean search operators.

Internet

Metasearching by Content

A **metasearch tool**, or **metasearch engine**, offers a single form to search a variety of powerful search engine indices simultaneously, based on keywords or phrases. These unified search interfaces provide a very powerful, convenient, and quick way to cover a lot of ground. ✎━━ To compare the differences between searching and metasearching, use a metasearch engine to check the major search engine indices simultaneously for the advantages of flat-panel monitors.

1. On the Student Online Companion, click the **Searching the Web folder**, then click the **Metasearching by content folder**

2. Click **Dogpile**

   The search form for Dogpile opens, as shown in Figure C-6. Notice that the search form for Dogpile contains a Search text box, and that there is a Fetch button to click to initiate the search.

3. Click the **Search text box**, then type **"flat panel monitor" advantages**

4. Click the **Fetch button**

   When the search is completed, Dogpile displays a listing of results collated by search engine, along with the total number of matches found. Note that Google may return a different number of matches using Dogpile than it did when directly queried in the previous lesson. Individual search engines often offer querying capabilities that are unavailable when using a metasearch site. To maximize your results, you should use individual search engines in conjunction with metasearch engines.

5. Scroll down the page to view the results

   The collated results for several search engines appear, as shown in Figure C-7.

6. Explore the links for two of the results, then return to the Student Online Companion

FIGURE C-6: Dogpile search form

Enter search terms here

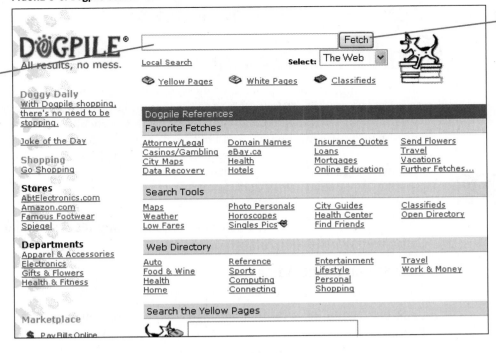

Click to submit search

FIGURE C-7: Dogpile's collated results from query

Search engine: Overture.com found 10 results. The query sent was +"flat panel monitor" +advantages

Partial list of results from one search engine

1. Compaq.com - Compaq TFT500 Flat Panel Monitor Key Technologies Paper
United States Compaq TFT500 Flat Panel Monitor Key Technologies Paper First Edition (May 1997) EMD069A/0696 Introduction This document describes the advantages and limitations of flat panel technology, Compaq TFT500 specifications, and the fut
www.compaq.com

2. Compare Prices on 15IN TFT 28MM 1024X768 FP FLAT TFT5010 LCD PANEL CARBON
The TFT5010 is designed to offer advanced flexibility for space-constrained environments and unparalleled image quality, complemented by all the advantages of digital technology, which gives users the highest level of image clarity of any flat...
www.pricegrabber.com

3. Introduction to Monitor & Flat Panel Display Technology
Hitachi America Ltd provides superior quality computer monitors and flat panel displays. These multi-award winning products range from 15 -21 inch models and carry some of the longest support hours in the industry.
www.hitachidisplays.com

4. Goldtouch - LCD Flat Panel Monitor
Goldtouch has extended its range of Ergonomic Desktop products, and is happy to offer another essential product for your computer desktop; the Goldtouch LCD Monitor.
www.goldtouch.com

5. New IBM 15-Inch Flat Panel Monitor Breaks $1,000 Barrier
New IBM 15-Inch Flat Panel Monitor Breaks $1,000 Barrier

Internet

Internet

Searching by Collection

Hundreds of thousands of Web sites already exist, and the number of sites continues to double nearly every two months. To help Web users find useful information about a topic, individuals and organizations that are interested in or dedicated to a particular subject create **collections**, or guides, which offer information and links to Web sites related to that subject. Some collections provide helpful overviews of the subject, in-depth articles, and insightful pointers to further resources. ⬤━ Intrigued by what you have found so far using search engines, find out more about how search engines work.

Steps 1 2 3 4

1. On the Student Online Companion, click the **Searching the Web folder**, then click the **Searching by collection folder**

2. Click **Search Engine Watch**
   A page with news, tips, and more about search engines appears, as shown in Figure C-8.

3. Click one of the links to another page about search engines (e.g., **Search Engine Resources**)
   A page like the one shown in Figure C-9 appears.

4. Scroll down the page, then click a link (e.g., **Search Engine Tutorials**)
   Figure C-10 shows a partial list of tutorials on search engine related topics.

5. Go back and explore some of the other links that interest you

6. When you have finished, return to the Student Online Companion

FIGURE C-8: Search Engine Watch page

FIGURE C-9: Search Engine Resources

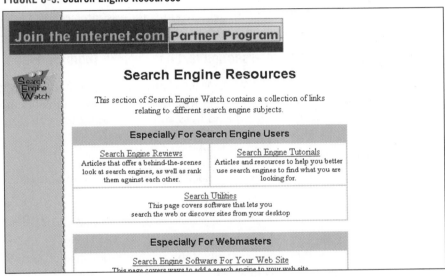

FIGURE C-10: Search Engine Tutorials

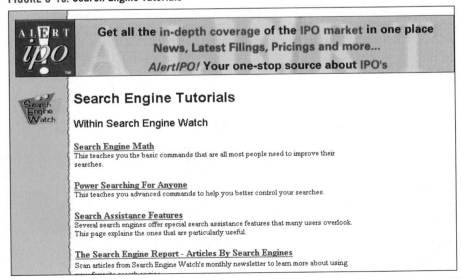

Searching for a Location

Internet

Two types of Web sites provide efficient ways of finding information related to a geographical area: map sites and location directories. A **map site** lets you specify an address and city or town and displays a map showing the location of the address you entered. Map sites are an excellent Web resource for locating places and learning where they are in relation to the surrounding area. You can also use a map site to create driving directions from one address to another. A **location directory** allows you to specify a geographical area and lists resources specific to that region. You're going to visit a friend who lives in Boston, Massachusetts. Before you head to Boston, find out which part of town she lives in, and print a map showing the area around her apartment.

Steps

1. On the Student Online Companion, click the **Searching the Web folder**, then click the **Searching for a location folder**

2. Click **MapQuest**
   The MapQuest page appears with fields to enter address/intersection, city, state, and zip code for U.S. addresses, as shown in Figure C-11.

3. Click in the **Address or Intersection text box**, type **25 Thomson Place**, then press **[Tab]**

4. In the City text box, type **Boston**, press **[Tab]**, then type **MA** in the State text box
   You only need to provide as much information as you have in the text boxes. Because you entered the city and state for the address you're searching for, you don't need to enter a zip code.

5. Click the **Map It! button**
   A partial map of Boston opens in the document window. A red star marks 25 Thomson Place, as shown in Figure C-12.

6. Scroll down if necessary to see the full map, then click the **ZOOM IN button** to the right of the map
   A new map opens, showing a close-up of the neighborhood around your friend's apartment, as shown in Figure C-13. Notice that less of the surrounding area is visible.

7. Experiment further with zooming in on and out of the map, then return to the Student Online Companion

Getting driving directions

In addition to showing maps of a single address, MapQuest and other map sites can provide driving directions between two locations. To get driving directions in MapQuest, enter an address and search for a map. On the results page, click Get Directions To This Location, enter the starting location and other specifications, then click Get Directions. The results page describes which roads to take and how far to travel on each before turning. Note that because map site directions are computer generated, it is always a good idea to double-check them against the map if possible to see if you are getting the best possible route.

FIGURE C-11: MapQuest search form

Enter address information in text boxes

Click to find a map for the address you entered

FIGURE C-12: Map results showing address you entered

Map of area surrounding the address you entered

Click to zoom in on map

Exact location of the address you entered

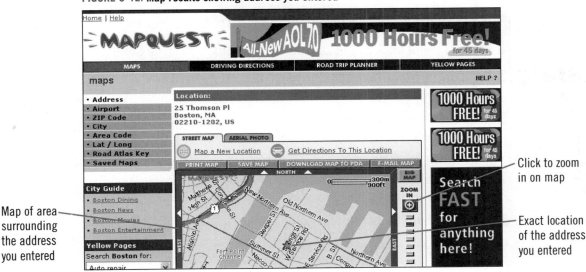

FIGURE C-13: Close-up of address you entered

Map showing closer view of area surrounding the address you entered

The address you entered remains marked at the center of the map

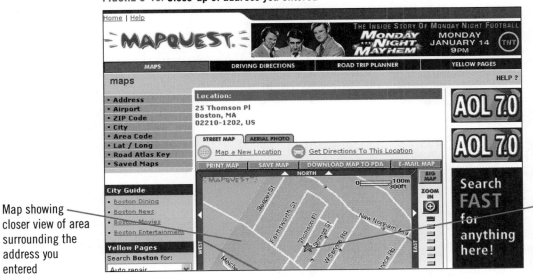

Internet

Unit C Internet

Searching for a Person

A people finder site assists you in locating some of the 30 million to 60 million people on the Internet. You can search for a person's e-mail address, Web page, and other contact information by name and other variables. Most people directories rely on the individual's name as the key search variable, while others let you specify query topics such as company, area, and college attended. ➤ While you're visiting your friend in Boston, you'd like to see if you can meet up with another friend there with whom you've lost contact. Use a people finder site to try to find this person's contact information.

Steps 1234

1. On the Student Online Companion, click the **Searching the Web folder**, then click the **Searching for a person folder**

2. Click **Switchboard**
   The initial page for the Switchboard appears with options for finding a person or business, as shown in Figure C-14.

3. In the Find a Person section, click in the **First Name text box**, then type **Jim**

4. Press **[Tab]** or click in the **Last Name text box**, then type **Smith**

5. Click in the **State text box**, then type **MA**
   Since you don't know the city where Jim lives, you leave the City text box empty.

6. Click the **Search button** in the Find a Person section
   A page appears listing the first 10 matches, as shown in Figure C-15.

7. Scroll down the page, then at the bottom of the page, click **Next Page**
   Because you think Jim lives somewhere near Boston, you can eliminate some of the returned addresses and then use the remaining listings to try to contact him.

8. Return to the Student Online Companion

QuickTip

If you have even a remote idea of the state or city where someone might be living, it's better to enter your guess because it will greatly narrow the results of your search. If the search fails to locate the person, you can always search again using another state or city.

FIGURE C-14: Switchboard home page

Enter information about person you're searching for in the Find a Person section

Click to submit search for a person

FIGURE C-15: Search results for Jim Smith

Details about matches to your search criteria

Unit C
Internet

Searching for Merchandise

The Web provides a convenient and efficient means for shopping for some items. The huge number of retailers selling goods and services on the Web, however, can make the thought of comparing prices and quality of service a daunting task. Many Web sites offer a comparison service for free, enabling you not only to identify sellers providing items you're looking for, but to view ratings of the sellers' reputations and reviews of the good or service you want to buy. You have decided to buy a flat-panel monitor. Use CNET.com to identify retailers selling these monitors online and to compare prices.

Steps

1. On the Student Online Companion, click the **Searching the Web folder**, then click the **Searching for merchandise folder**

2. Click **CNET**
   The CNET.com home page appears.

3. If necessary, scroll down, then click **Latest Prices**
   The Latest Prices page opens, listing categories of merchandise for which CNET tracks latest prices.

4. If necessary, scroll down, then click **Monitors**
   The Monitors page opens, displaying links by monitor category and brand, as shown in Figure C-16.

5. Click **Flat-panel displays**, then click **17-in. to 21-in. flat-panel displays**
   A list of 17-in. to 21-in. flat-panel monitors appears, sorted by manufacturer name.

6. Click **Sort by Price**, then scroll down to see the list
   The list is reordered by price, with the least expensive monitor at the top of the list, as shown in Figure C-17.

7. Click the name of the first monitor in the list
   A page opens containing product specifications and ratings, if available. Further down the page is a table listing online vendors that sell this model, along with their most recently reported price, and CNET's rating of the seller.

8. Close Internet Explorer

FIGURE C-16: Monitors page on CNET.com

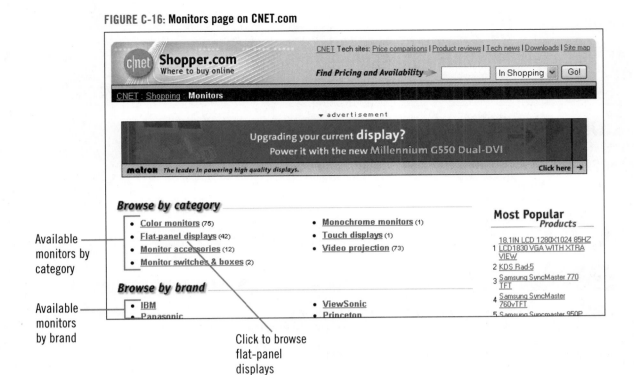

Available monitors by category

Available monitors by brand

Click to browse flat-panel displays

FIGURE C-17: List of 17-in. to 21-in. flat-panel monitors sorted by price

Click to view specifications and prices for least expensive model

Sort by Company Name		Sort by Price	Most Popular Products
Samsung Electronics Co. Ltd. SyncMaster 700 IFT POP Samsung Electronics Co. Ltd.		▶ **Check Latest Prices** Lowest price: $188	18.1IN LCD 1280X1024 85HZ 1 LCD1830 VGA WITH XTRA VIEW
LG Electronics Flatron 795FT Plus POP LG Electronics U.S.A. Inc.		▶ **Check Latest Prices** Lowest price: $218	2 KDS Rad-5 3 Samsung SyncMaster 770 TFT
ViewSonic Optiquest Q95 POP ViewSonic Corp.		▶ **Check Latest Prices** Lowest price: $219	4 Samsung SyncMaster 760vTFT 5 Samsung Syncmaster 950P
Samsung Electronics Co. Ltd. SyncMaster 900 IFT POP Samsung Electronics Co. Ltd.		▶ **Check Latest Prices** Lowest price: $302	**Top 50 Monitors**
Apple Studio Display POP Apple Computer		▶ **Check Latest Prices** Lowest price: $459	CNET *Tech Auctions*
Envision EN-7100e 🔲Editors' Choice POP Envision Peripherals		▶ **Check Latest Prices** Lowest price: $549	**Sony 32M Vid 20-inch** Starting bid: $9 **Futura .25 19inchFST** Starting bid: $1
ViewSonic VG 175 POP ViewSonic Corp.		▶ **Check Latest Prices** Lowest price: $558	**LaCie .24dp 22-inch** Starting bid: $969 **Sony .28dp 20-inch** Starting bid: $9
Samsung SyncMaster 760vTFT POP		▶ **Check Latest Prices**	PythonRadeon 64M AGP

List of 17-in. to 21-in. flat-panel monitors sorted by price

Internet

Practice

► Concepts Review

Describe each option of the Google Web page shown in Figure C-18.

FIGURE C-18

Match each term with the statement that best describes its function.

6. Yahoo!   a. Collection
7. Dogpile   b. People finder
8. Search Engine Watch   c. Product index
9. CNET Latest Prices   d. Metasearch engine
10. Switchboard   e. Subject directory

Select the best answer from the list of choices.

11. **Which of the following are NOT search tools?**
    a. Subject directories
    b. Cards
    c. Metasearch engines
    d. Collections

12. **Which of the following is NOT a Web search strategy?**
    a. Browse collections
    b. Search generally at first
    c. Search using a dictionary
    d. Narrow your search with search engines

13. **Google on the Web is a:**
    a. Search engine.
    b. Location listing.
    c. Metasearch engine.
    d. Phone directory.

14. **Dogpile is a:**
    a. Collection.
    b. Metasearch engine.
    c. Search engine.
    d. Companion for finding Internet protocols.

15. **Google lets you search by:**
    a. Merchandise.
    b. Content.
    c. Latitude and longitude.
    d. Collection.

16. **MapQuest lets you search for a(n):**
    a. Index.
    b. Password.
    c. Location.
    d. Collection.

17. **When you search with Dogpile, it returns results from:**
    a. The Dogpile search engine.
    b. One other randomly selected search engine.
    c. Multiple other search engines.
    d. Dogpile is a subject directory, not a search tool.

18. Map sites often also provide:
   a. Maps through the mail.
   b. Airline reservations.
   c. Driving directions.
   d. Forms for searching for people.

19. A metasearch engine works by:
   a. Searching a variety of metafiles at the same time.
   b. Querying a variety of search engine indices simultaneously.
   c. Querying the best online dictionaries.
   d. Searching for an exact phrase in a URL.

► Skills Review

1. Search by subject.
   a. Open Internet Explorer, type **www.course.com/downloads/illustrated/ie6** in the Address text box on the Address bar, then press [Enter].
   b. On the Student Online Companion, click the Searching the Web folder, then click the Searching by subject folder.
   c. Click the link for a subject directory other than the one you used in the unit.
   d. Select a category such as "Recreation" or "Sports," and narrow the subject to the sport of soccer.
   e. Find resources about soccer.
   f. Click the link for one Web page about soccer.
   g. Return to the Student Online Companion.

2. Search by content.
   a. On the Student Online Companion, click the Searching the Web folder, then click the Searching by content folder.
   b. Click the link for a search engine other than the one you used in the unit.
   c. Search for the phrase **"indoor soccer"** (include the quotation marks).
   d. Examine the first two pages of results, then click the link for one of the results.
   e. Return to the Student Online Companion.

3. Metasearch by content.
   a. On the Student Online Companion, open the Searching the Web folder, then open the Metasearching by content folder.
   b. Click the link for a metasearch engine other than the one you used in the unit.
   c. Search on the phrase **"indoor soccer"** (include the quotation marks).
   d. Examine the results returned by at least two different search engines, then click the link for one of the results.
   e. Return to the Student Online Companion.

4. **Search by collection.**
   a. On the Student Online Companion, open the Searching the Web folder, then open the Searching by collection folder.
   b. Click the link for a collection other than the one you used in the unit.
   c. Read the most recent article or news item you can find about the collection's subject.
   d. Return to the Student Online Companion.

5. **Search for a location.**
   a. On the Student Online Companion, open the Searching the Web folder, then open the Searching for a location folder.
   b. Click the link for a location resource other than the one you used in the unit.
   c. If you selected a map site, enter your home address, city, and state, view the map of your surrounding area, then zoom out to see a wider view of your vicinity.
   d. If you selected a site that provides information about geographical regions, navigate to information about your state, province, or territory, then click one link to information about your area.
   e. Return to the Student Online Companion.

6. **Search for a person.**
   a. On the Student Online Companion, open the Searching the Web folder, then open the Searching for a person folder.
   b. Click the link for a people search resource other than the one you used in the unit, then, if necessary, navigate to a search form on the site.
   c. Enter the name, city, and state for yourself or one of your family members or friends, then search for information about the person you entered.
   d. Return to the Student Online Companion.

7. **Search for Merchandise.**
   a. On the Student Online Companion, open the Searching the Web folder, then open the Searching for merchandise folder.
   b. Click the link for a merchandise search resource other than the one you used in the unit.
   c. Use the Web site you opened to find the lowest price for a cell phone.
   d. Close Internet Explorer.

Internet

Independent Challenge 1

You are beginning your first week as a columnist for a new magazine dedicated to covering business on the Web. You want to familiarize yourself with the current issues in electronic commerce.

a. On the Student Online Companion (www.course.com/downloads/illustrated/ie6), open the Searching the Web folder, then the Searching by subject folder.

b. Click Yahoo!, click the Business & Economy category, then click the Business to Business link.

c. Click Electronic Commerce.

d. Explore two of the topics under Electronic Commerce.

e. Using a word-processing program, write a separate paragraph summarizing each subtopic to bring to the magazine's next issue-planning meeting, scheduled for later in the week. Be sure to add your name to the top of the document.

Independent Challenge 2

You're interested in exploring cooking-related links and resources available on the Web. Start by using a Web collection that a friend referred you to.

a. On the Student Online Companion (www.course.com/downloads/illustrated/ie6), click the Searching the Web folder, then click the Searching by collection folder.

b. Click The Kitchen Link and examine the site's home page.

c. Explore three links in different categories on the site's home page.

d. Using a word-processing program, write a paragraph describing the types of cooking-related resources available online. Be sure to add your name to the top of the document.

▶ Independent Challenge 3

After speaking with a Peace Corps representative and reviewing the large packet of information mailed to you, you discover you are eligible for several teaching positions open in South Africa. You know very little about this country, so you decide to use a location directory to find out more about it.

a. On the Student Online Companion, click the Searching the Web folder, click the Searching for a location folder, then click Travel Library.

b. Use this site to find the following information about South Africa:

- A map of the country.
- Its climate.
- Its currency.
- Two other facts that would be important for a visitor to know in advance.

c. Using a word-processing program, write a few paragraphs summarizing the information you find. Be sure to type your name on the document before printing.

▶ Independent Challenge 4

John Prescott, your boss at Words and Wisdom bookstore, is planning trips to two literary meetings at libraries in other cities. Use the skills you learned in this unit to print area maps of the following locations in the United States:

101 N. Stone, Tucson, AZ

300 Nicollet Mall, Minneapolis, MN

Internet

▶ Visual Workshop

Use the skills you learned in this unit to locate a Web page that explains the history of the Linux operating system, similar to the page shown in Figure C-19. Print a copy of the page.

FIGURE C-19

What is Linux

Linux is an operating system that was initially created as a hobby by a young student, Linus Torvalds, at the University of Helsinki in Finland. Linus had an interest in Minix, a small UNIX system, and decided to develop a system that exceeded the Minix standards. He began his work in 1991 when he released version 0.02 and worked steadily until 1994 when version 1.0 of the Linux Kernel was released. The current full-featured version is 2.4 (released January 2001) and development continues.

Linux is developed under the GNU General Public License and its source code is freely available to everyone. This however, doesn't mean that Linux and its assorted distributions are free -- companies and developers may charge money for it as long as the source code remains available. Linux may be used for a wide variety of purposes including networking, software development, and as an end-user platform. Linux is often considered an excellent, low-cost alternative to other more expensive operating systems.

Due to the very nature of Linux's functionality and availability, it has become quite popular worldwide and a vast number of software programmers have taken Linux's source code and adapted it to meet their individual needs. At this time, there are dozens of ongoing projects for porting Linux to various hardware configurations and purposes.

Linux has an official mascot, the Linux Penguin, which was selected by Linus Torvalds to represent the image he associates with the operating system he created.

Exploring
the Web

Objectives

- ► **Understand categories of information on the Web**
- ► **Explore electronic commerce**
- ► **Explore employment**
- ► **Explore Web media**
- ► **Explore entertainment**
- ► **Explore government**
- ► **Explore portals**
- ► **Explore online help**

Once you know how to navigate and search the World Wide Web, you can explore the resources available on the Web. Although the information available on the Web can be categorized in almost limitless ways, you can pick a few of the most common areas to begin understanding and experiencing the breadth of what's available online. ✐ In this unit, you'll explore some of the major types of resources available on the Web.

Internet

Understanding Categories of Information on the Web

Understanding the types of information available on the Web makes it easier to locate information of interest to you. The list below summarizes several of the most popular categories of Web resources. This list is nowhere near a comprehensive representation of Web content. The Web includes many other types of information, such as those listed in the Google directory shown in Figure D-1. However, the list below describes some of the most useful and frequently visited types of sites. 🖋 The main categories of information on the Web that you'll be exploring include:

Details

▶ **Electronic commerce:** online business transactions, electronic payment systems, and online shopping

▶ **Employment:** jobs and career information

▶ **Web media:** online magazines, newspapers, and television and radio station resources

▶ **Entertainment:** art, movies, music, and TV

▶ **Portals:** links and tools to help you find useful Web resources

▶ **Government:** U.S. government directories, branches, departments, and independent establishments

▶ **Online help:** technical assistance for software and computer accessories

	Google Search	· Directory Help

The web organized by topic into categories.

Arts
Movies, Music, Television,...

Home
Consumers, Homeowners, Family,...

Regional
Asia, Europe, North America,...

Business
Industries, Finance, Jobs,...

Kids and Teens
Computers, Entertainment, School,...

Science
Biology, Psychology, Physics,...

Computers
Hardware, Internet, Software,...

News
Media, Newspapers, Current Events,...

Shopping
Autos, Clothing, Gifts,...

Games
Board, Roleplaying, Video,...

Recreation
Food, Outdoors, Travel,...

Society
Issues, People, Religion,...

Health
Alternative, Fitness, Medicine,...

Reference
Education, Libraries, Maps,...

Sports
Basketball, Football, Soccer,...

World
Deutsch, Español, Français, Italiano, Japanese, Korean, Nederlands, Polska, Svenska, ...

CLUES TO USE

Web statistics and demographics

Estimates of the number of Internet users range from 300 million to 400 million. Browsing the Web is second only to e-mail as the most popular activity on the Internet. The number of Web pages totals over a billion.

For more information and resources on these topics and on the demographics of Web users, click Statistics and demographics under the About the Web heading on the Student Online Companion.

Internet

Exploring Electronic Commerce

Electronic commerce, or **e-commerce**, is the process of transacting business online. This type of commerce primarily consists of business-to-business and business-to-consumer transactions. In a **Business-to-Business**—or **B2B**—transaction, a business or other organization orders supplies, equipment, or other goods electronically from another business. Most Web users are more likely to take part in a **Business-to-Consumer**—or **B2C**—transaction, in which an individual purchases products or services using the Web. Both types of transactions share many concerns, such as security, electronic payment systems, and reliability. ✐ Explore the process of shopping online at the Web site of a large bookstore.

1. Open Internet Explorer, type **www.course.com/downloads/illustrated/ie6** in the Address text box on the Address bar, then press **[Enter]**
   The Student Online Companion for this book opens in the document window.

2. Click the **Exploring the Web folder**, then click the **Exploring electronic commerce folder**
   A list of links to e-commerce sites appears.

Trouble?

If *powells.com* is unavailable, use another resource from the Exploring electronic commerce folder to look at online shopping.

3. Click **powells.com**
   The Web site for Powell's bookstore opens, as shown in Figure D-2. This site sells used, new, and out-of-print books over the Web.

4. In the **Search text box**, type **James Baldwin**, then click **Search**
   A page opens listing books by or about James Baldwin that are available on *powells.com*.

5. Click the title of one of the books listed
   A description of the book appears.

6. Click **Add to Shopping Cart**
   The shopping cart page opens listing the items that you have selected to buy, as shown in Figure D-3. The shopping cart page is popular on Web stores, enabling users to view at any time the items they have chosen and to put some back if they wish. The shopping cart page allows you to continue shopping or to proceed to checkout, where you pay for the items you've chosen.

7. Click **checkout**
   A Web page opens describing the security measures that this Web site uses to ensure that your checkout information is safe. The page also gives instructions on how to proceed to complete the transaction. If you were going to continue with this purchase, you would provide your name, address, and credit card information on subsequent pages. Because shipping can be a considerable expense for customers buying products online, reputable online shopping sites show you the total amount of your purchase, including shipping, before you complete the transaction.

QuickTip

To return to the Student Online Companion, use the Back button, the History list, or enter the following URL in the Address text box: *www.course.com/downloads/illustrated/ie6*

8. Return to the Student Online Companion

FIGURE D-2: **Home page at powells.com**

Browsable categories of books

Click to submit search on author, title, or subject

Enter terms to search for

FIGURE D-3: **Shopping cart page at powells.com**

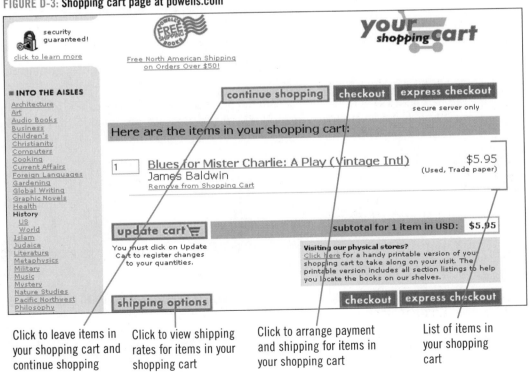

Click to leave items in your shopping cart and continue shopping

Click to view shipping rates for items in your shopping cart

Click to arrange payment and shipping for items in your shopping cart

List of items in your shopping cart

Internet

Unit D
Internet

Exploring Employment

The Internet has become an indispensable medium for many of today's technology-savvy job seekers and recruiters. In addition to the customary job listings section at most commercial Web sites, a number of sites specialize in helping employers and job seekers find each other. Along with job-listing services, these employment sites typically offer assistance with career planning and resume preparation. ✒ Explore the features and resources available at a popular Web site for employment.

Steps 1234

1. On the Student Online Companion, click the **Exploring the Web folder**, then click the **Exploring employment folder**
A list of links to employment sites appears.

Trouble?
If Monster.com is unavailable, use another resource from the Exploring employment folder to look at job listings on the Web.

2. Click **Monster**
The home page for Monster.com appears, as shown in Figure D-4. The Monster.com Web site lists jobs available in the United States and internationally, with a special search agent that automatically locates positions matching your interests and qualifications. Monster also provides a career center to help you hone your resume, a database to search for company information, and advice on relocation and career management.

3. Click the **Search Jobs** link
The Job Search page displays a search form that enables you to enter job and location information.

4. Scroll down in the Location Search list box until **Washington-Seattle** appears, then click it
The Washington-Seattle selection appears highlighted.

5. Scroll down in the Job Category Search list box until **Arts, Entertainment, and Media** appears, then click it
The category selection appears highlighted, as shown in Figure D-5. You can alternately use the Keyword Search text box to look for types of jobs not listed in the Job Category Search list box.

Trouble?
If no positions are currently available in the chosen location, return to the search form, click another location (e.g., California-San Jose), then repeat the search.

6. Scroll down the page, then click the **Search Jobs button**
The results appear on a new page, similar to Figure D-6.

7. Click one of the job postings
A page with information about a job listing appears.

8. Examine the information that is available for the position (e.g., duties, responsibilities, and qualifications)

9. Go back to the results list, explore another posting, then return to the Student Online Companion

FIGURE D-4: Monster home page

Click to search the jobs database

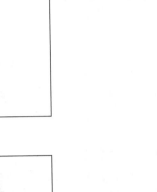

FIGURE D-5: Job search parameters selected

Location selected

Job category selected

FIGURE D-6: Example of search results

Jobs that match the location and job category specified

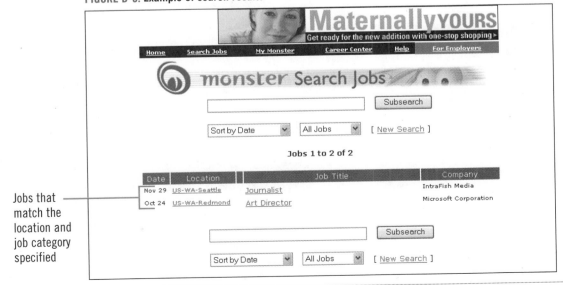

Exploring Web Media

Many newspapers and magazines offer part, or all, of their print content on the Web. Many of the major television networks and large individual television and radio stations also have Web presences where they make news stories and media clips available. Additionally, online-only news outlets, known as **Web zines** (short for Web magazines), have established themselves as part of the media world. Web zines range from a few large and well-known sites, like *salon.com*, to thousands of smaller ones on topics that appeal to a narrow readership. Investigate the content of the online version of a print newspaper and of a Web zine.

1. On the Student Online Companion, click the **Exploring the Web folder**, then click the **Exploring Web media folder**

2. Click **The New York Times**

   The home page for The New York Times appears, as shown in Figure D-7. The paper's title appears in the same font as the title of the newspaper's print version. If The New York Times is unavailable, use another resource from the Exploring Web media folder to look at traditional media on the Web.

3. Click the headline for one of the main stories

   The story opens, as shown in Figure D-8. The Web page includes a couple of icons that can facilitate sharing the article with other people. The Printer-Friendly Format icon opens a new page showing the story in a layout that better fits on printed pages. The E-Mail This Article icon opens a form that enables you to e-mail the story to someone you know.

4. Return to the Student Online Companion, click the **Exploring the Web folder**, click the **Exploring Web media folder**, then click **salon.com**

5. Scroll down the page to view the headlines and other feaures

   Figure D-9 shows the home page for salon.com.

6. Click the headline for one of the main articles

   The article opens.

7. Read the article, then return to the Student Online Companion

> ### Trouble?
>
> If a Web page opens asking for a username and password, fill in the necessary fields in the Register Now section to create a new username and password, or just examine Figure D-8 and go on to Step 4.

FIGURE D-7: The New York Times on the Web home page

Links to main stories

FIGURE D-8: Article on The New York Times Web site

Click to e-mail this article to a friend or colleague

Text of article from print edition

Click to display the page without side-bars, for easier readability when printed

FIGURE D-9: Salon.com home page

Headlines of current articles

Recent articles grouped by topic

Unit D — Internet

Exploring Entertainment

The interactive nature of the Web allows you to access many types of traditional entertainment in a single medium. For example, virtual art collections, galleries, and museums on the Web feature digital representations of the world's greatest pieces of artwork. Promotional movie sites are stocked with film-related goodies such as downloadable posters and video clips. Additionally, music sites let you discuss and listen to your favorite bands. ✒️ Explore how traditional entertainment has adapted to the Web by visiting a Web museum.

Steps

1. On the Student Online Companion, click the **Exploring the Web folder**, then click the **Exploring entertainment folder**

2. Click **ArtNet**
   The home page for ArtNet appears, as shown in Figure D-10.

Trouble?

If ArtNet is unavailable, use another resource from the Exploring entertainment folder to look at entertainment options on the Web.

3. Click **artists** at the top of the page
   The Artist Index opens, as shown in Figure D-11. The page allows you to search for an artist's works by the artist's last name.

4. Click the letter **R** at the top of the page
   A list of artists with last names starting with R opens.

5. Scroll down and click the link **Rivera, Diego**
   A page opens showing available works by Diego Rivera in galleries that are members of ArtNet, as shown in Figure D-12.

6. Click one of the images
   A larger graphic of the artwork you clicked opens in the document window.

7. Review the image and the available information about the image, then return to the Student Online Companion

CLUES TO USE

Web ethics and law

The question of Web developers' responsibilities and rights regarding the content they make available on their Web sites has produced an ongoing debate. This question is both an ethical and legal one. For information on the ethical issues, click the About the Web folder in the Student Online Companion, click the Ethics folder, then click one of the links. To find out about U.S. legislative bills affecting these legal issues, click the Exploring the Web folder, click the Exploring government folder, then click Thomas—Legislative Information. Use the Thomas site to search for bills pending or passed about online copyrights and other Web content issues.

FIGURE D-10: ArtNet home page

Click to open an index of artists

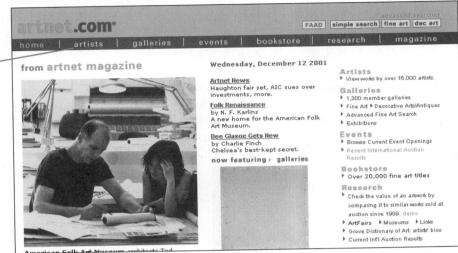

FIGURE D-11: Artist index page on ArtNet

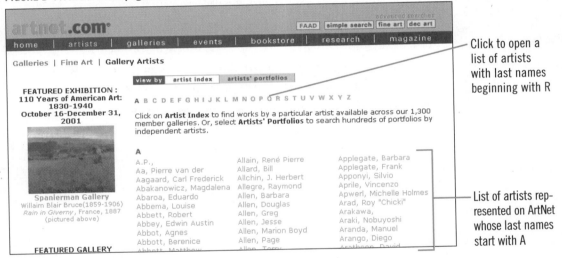

Click to open a list of artists with last names beginning with R

List of artists represented on ArtNet whose last names start with A

FIGURE D-12: Works by Diego Rivera

Click an image to view a full-screen graphic of the artwork

Internet

Unit D
Internet

Exploring Government

Many governments around the world use the Web to provide information and services to residents and visitors. Government Web sites can be a useful source of basic information about government policies and programs and a research tool for looking up laws, statements, and official acts. Use U.S. federal government resources available on the Web to learn about Social Security benefits available to American retirees.

Trouble?

If you cannot connect to the FirstGov Web site, click another link from the Exploring the government folder (such as FedWorld), and use it to explore U.S. government resources available online.

1. On the Student Online Companion, click the **Exploring the Web folder**, then click the **Exploring government folder**

2. Click **FirstGov**
The home page for FirstGov opens, as shown in Figure D-13. FirstGov provides categorized links to U.S. federal government information available on the Web.

3. Scroll down to review the page, then click **Benefits and Grants**
The Benefits and Grants page opens.

4. Scroll down, then click **Social Security** under the Featured Links heading
The Social Security Administration home page opens, as shown in Figure D-14.

5. Click **Retirement** on the left side of the page under the Benefits Information heading
The Social Security Retirement page opens, as shown in Figure D-15.

6. Explore the page, then return to the Student Online Companion

FIGURE D-13: FirstGov home page

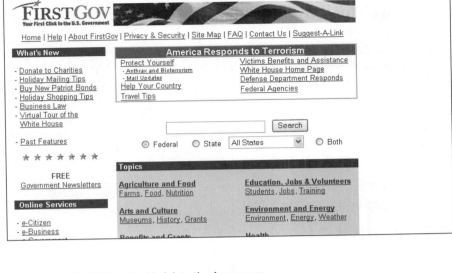

FIGURE D-14: Social Security Administration home page

Link to information on retirement benefits

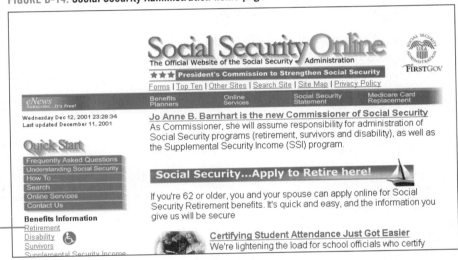

FIGURE D-15: Social Security Administration retirement page

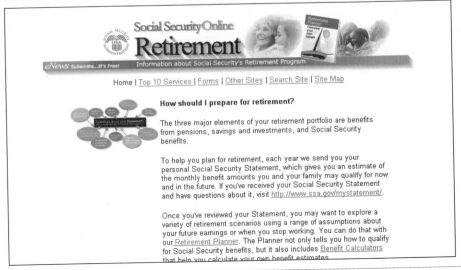

Unit D

Internet

Exploring Portals

A **portal** is a Web site that provides a centralized, and potentially customized, set of options for using the Web all in one place. A Web portal generally incorporates a search engine and a directory, news headlines, and other features to encourage users to return, such as e-mail access and other personalized content. Portal users can customize page layout and content to display items they select—including specific news subjects and links to certain resources they use frequently. Major portals on the Web today include search engines such as Yahoo!, AltaVista, and Lycos, as well as the start pages for makers of widely-used Web software, such as the Netscape Netcenter and Microsoft's MSN. To better understand the features and advantages of using a Web portal, explore the Yahoo! site.

1. On the Student Online Companion, click the **Exploring the Web folder**, then click the **Exploring portals folder**

2. Click **Yahoo!**
   The initial page for Yahoo! opens, as shown in Figure D-16.

3. Click **Personalize** at the top of the page
   The My Yahoo! page opens, as shown in Figure D-17.

Trouble?

If you don't have a Yahoo! ID and password, click the Sign Up Now button and complete the necessary fields to set up a Yahoo! account, or just read the steps and view the associated figures.

4. Enter your Yahoo! ID and password in the Sign in to Yahoo! section on the left side of the Web page, then click **Sign in**
   A My Yahoo! page like the one shown in Figure D-18 opens. The content of this page is customized based on your registration information.

5. Scroll down the default My Yahoo! page for your account
   The information displayed includes weather for your area, news headlines, sports scores, and information based on any interests you indicated while registering.

Trouble?

If there is no Scoreboard section on your customized page, click the Close button in a different section.

6. Click the **Close button** in the Scoreboard section
   A confirmation window opens, asking if you're sure you want to remove this module from the Web page.

7. Click **OK** in the dialog box

8. Scroll down the page to view the updated content
   The Scoreboard section no longer appears on your My Yahoo! page. You can remove additional sections in the same way. You can also change colors, content, and layout using the buttons at the top of the page, as well as add additional pages to your personalized portal.

9. When you have finished, click **Sign Out**, then return to the Student Online Companion

FIGURE D-16: Yahoo! portal home page

Click to personalize content on your Yahoo! home page

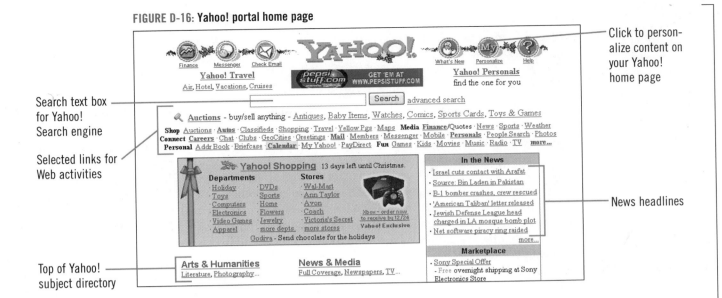

Search text box for Yahoo! Search engine

Selected links for Web activities

News headlines

Top of Yahoo! subject directory

FIGURE D-17: My Yahoo! page

Enter ID and password to sign in to Yahoo!

FIGURE D-18: Customized My Yahoo! page

Use buttons to change, add, or remove content

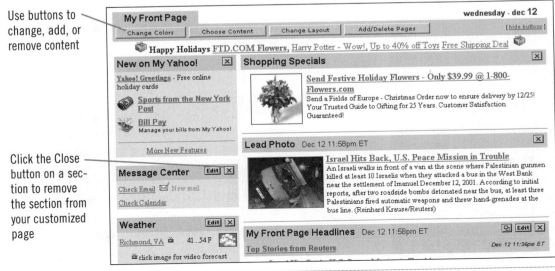

Click the Close button on a section to remove the section from your customized page

Exploring Online Help

Many software makers, as well as manufacturers of computers and computer accessories, offer extensive help resources on their Web sites. While saving companies the expense of responding to users' queries by phone or e-mail, Web-based technical support also allows users to answer their own questions without sitting on hold on the phone or waiting for a reply to an e-mail. Most online help sites include a searchable database of issues that other users have encountered. A site might also include forums where users can help each other with problems, automated troubleshooters that step users through possible solutions to a problem, and phone and e-mail contact information, in case the online offerings aren't enough to solve the problem. Investigate online help offerings at the Microsoft Web site that might address a problem that a friend is having with Windows.

Steps

1. On the Student Online Companion, click the **Exploring the Web folder**, then click the **Exploring online help folder**

2. Click **Microsoft Help and Support**
   The Microsoft Help and Support home page appears, as shown in Figure D-19.

3. Click the list arrow in the Search text box, then click **Windows 2000** if necessary

4. Click in the **For solutions containing... text box**, then type **lost password**

5. Click the **Search now arrow**
   A search results page opens, listing possible matches for your query, as shown in Figure D-20.

6. Scroll down the page to view the search results, then click the link to one of the articles listed
   The article opens in its own browser window, as shown in Figure D-21. If the listed articles don't directly address your problem, you can provide more information in the fields at the top of the search results Web page in order to find more relevant articles.

7. Close the browser window containing the article, then close Internet Explorer

Customer service on the Web

In addition to facilitating technical support, the Web also provides a platform for providing and accessing traditional customer service options. Companies and other organizations can make information such as account statements and product manuals available to customers online. Making such resources available on the Web reduces costs for organizations providing them. At the same time, accessing information online reduces customer wait times in lines or on hold on a telephone. Web-based customer service options are also accessible 24 hours a day, providing access at the user's convenience, rather than restricting it to set hours. Many organizations have implemented online customer service in a variety of applications. For example, customers of Federal Express, the United Parcel Service, and the U.S. Postal Service can check on the location and delivery status of shipped packages by entering a tracking code on each organization's Web site. The U.S. Postal Service Web site also enables users to find the ZIP code for a given address and to calculate postage rates online. Many banks and credit card companies also allow their customers to access their account statements and recent transactions through a secure Web server.

FIGURE D-19: Microsoft Help and Support home page

Category and
search terms
entered

Click to submit
search

FIGURE D-20: Search results in Microsoft Help and Support

Options for
narrowing
search results

Suggested help
topics based on
your search
terms

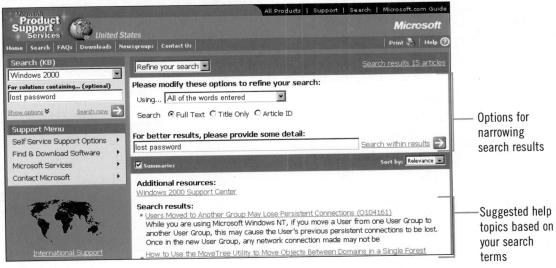

FIGURE D-21: Sample article returned in response to query

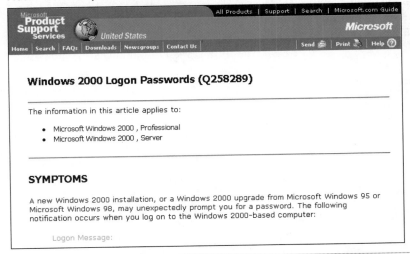

Internet

Practice

▶ Concepts Review

Label the types of Web portal offerings indicated in Figure D-22.

FIGURE D-22

Match each of the terms below with the statement that best describes its function.

6. **Electronic commerce**
7. **Online help**
8. **Web media**
9. **Portal**

a. Web-based answers to technical questions
b. Web page offering customized access to many Web resources
c. Online business transactions
d. Web presence of newspapers, magazines, and TV networks

Select the best answer from the list of choices.

10. **The New York Times on the Web is an example of:**
    a. Government online.
    b. Web media.
    c. Online help.
    d. An employment resource.

11. **Which of the following do portals generally NOT offer?**
    a. A search engine
    b. A directory
    c. News
    d. Recipes

12. **Online shopping sites generally include a(n):**
    a. Portal.
    b. Bargain bin.
    c. Shopping cart.
    d. Online magazine.

13. **When a business buys supplies or equipment electronically, the transaction is an example of which kind of commerce?**
    a. B2C
    b. B2D
    c. Business to Consumer
    d. Business to Business

Internet

▶ Skills Review

1. **Explore electronic commerce.**
   a. Open Internet Explorer, type **www.course.com/downloads/illustrated/ie6** in the Address text box on the Address bar, then press [Enter].
   b. On the Student Online Companion, click the Exploring the Web folder, then click the Exploring electronic commerce folder.
   c. Click eBay.
   d. In the what are you looking for? text box, type **acoustic guitar**, then click find it.
   e. When the search results appear, scroll down and review the first page of listings, then click the link for one of the guitars for sale.
   f. Return to the Student Online Companion.

2. **Explore employment.**
   a. On the Student Online Companion, click the Exploring the Web folder, then click the Exploring employment folder.
   b. Click Helpwanted.com.
   c. Click Job Seeker, then click Search By Profession on the page that opens.
   d. When the search form appears, click Computer/Information Technology in the Profession list box, then click the Web Development check box under the Specialty heading.
   e. Select USA as the country, Washington as the state, and Seattle as the city, then click Search Jobs.
   f. Explore the search results. (*Note*: If no Computer/Information Technology Web development positions are available for Seattle, return to the search form and enter another city and state, such as Los Angeles, California.)
   g. Return to the Student Online Companion.

3. **Explore Web media.**
   a. On the Student Online Companion, click the Exploring the Web folder, then click the Exploring Web media folder.
   b. Click HotWired.
   c. Find and read a news article on the HotWired page that interests you.
   d. Return to the Student Online Companion.

4. **Explore entertainment.**
   a. On the Student Online Companion, click the Exploring the Web folder, then click the Exploring entertainment folder.
   b. Click The Internet Movie Database.
   c. Type **Wizard of Oz** in the Search the database for text box, then click the Go button.
   d. Explore the results to find out who directed the 1939 release of *The Wizard of Oz*.
   e. Return to the Student Online Companion.

5. **Explore government.**
   a. On the Student Online Companion, click the Exploring the Web folder, then click the Exploring government folder.
   b. Click Thomas—Legislative Information.
   c. Type **Internet** in the Search by Word/Phrase text box, then click the Search button.
   d. Explore one of the bills listed in the search results.
   e. Return to the Student Online Companion.

6. Explore portals.

  a. On the Student Online Companion, click the Exploring the Web folder, then click the Exploring portals folder.

  b. Click Netscape.

  c. Click My Netscape at the top of the page.

  d. Click the Layout button under the Personalize heading at the top of the page.

  e. If you have a Netscape Netcenter Screen name and password, sign in; otherwise, click Sign Up as a New Netscape Member and create a new account, or simply read the remaining steps.

  f. Click the Layout button again under the Personalize heading at the top of the page.

  g. In the Left Column box, click Sports, click the up arrow twice to move it to the top of the list, then click Save.

  h. Notice the new arrangement of your Netscape page.

  i. Return to the Student Online Companion.

7. Explore online help.

  a. On the Student Online Companion, click the Exploring the Web folder, then click the Exploring online help folder.

  b. Click Adobe Customer Support.

  c. Click Support by product, then in the window that opens, click Acrobat Reader.

  d. Select the topic Configuring Web Browsers with Acrobat Reader, then click Continue.

  e. Scroll down to view the preliminary documents that Adobe Online Help makes available.

  f. Close Internet Explorer.

Independent Challenge 1

The PR firm Words and Wisdom is growing rapidly. John Prescott realizes that he needs to be able to conduct business online. He asks you to experiment with the electronic payment systems for other online businesses.

    a. On the Student Online Companion (www.course.com/downloads/illustrated/ie6), click the Exploring the Web folder, then click the Exploring electronic commerce folder.

    b. Click *amazon.com*.

    c. Explore the site and place a product in your shopping cart.

    d. Proceed to checkout until you reach the page that asks you for a credit card number.

    e. Using a word-processing program, write a description of each page you encountered when checking out; note the specific information requested on each page. Be sure to include your name at the top of the document.

 # Independent Challenge 2

Your history professor has assigned research topics for the final paper. Your paper will discuss the history of 10 Downing Street, the residence of the British prime minister. You decide to use the Web to research your paper.

    a. On the Student Online Companion (www.course.com/downloads/illustrated/ie6), click the Exploring the Web folder, then click the Exploring government folder.

    b. Click 10 Downing Street.

    c. Click the 10 out of 10 link at the bottom of the left toolbar, then click History.

    d. Click History of the Building, then review the history of 10 Downing Street.

    e. Print a copy of the most interesting page in the History of the Building section. Add your name to the printout.

▶ Independent Challenge 3

You have applied to and been accepted by an art school in Paris, France, and you leave next month. You want to familiarize yourself with art galleries in Paris before you leave. Use the ArtNet link in the Exploring entertainment folder on the Student Online Companion (www.course.com/downloads/illustrated/ie6) to learn more about art galleries in Paris. Print a copy of the most interesting gallery you find. Add your name to the printout.

▶ Independent Challenge 4

Find out what local media is available via the Web for the place you live or for someplace you have visited or would like to visit. If necessary, use a search engine or Web directory to find the names of at least one local newspaper and two television or radio stations serving the area you're researching. (For a list of search engines, click the Searching the Web folder on the Student Online Companion (www.course.com/downloads/illustrated/ie6), then click Searching by content. For a list of directories, click the Searching the Web folder, then click Searching by subject.) Using a search engine, search for the newspaper's name. If a link to it appears in the search results, open its Web site and print the home page. Repeat this process for both television or radio stations.

► **Visual Workshop**

Use the skills you learned in this unit to find and print the digitized artwork shown in Figure D-23 or another artwork by the same artist. (*Hint*: The artist's name is M.C. Escher.) Add your name to the printout.

FIGURE D-23

Glossary

Internet

Address Bar Toolbar that displays the URL for the current Web page and enables entry of a URL to open a Web page in the document window. *See also* Uniform Resource Locator (URL).

Address text box Displays the address of the Web page shown in the Internet Explorer document window.

Applet A program included in a Web page that usually enables the page to interact with users. However, some applets can be security risks.

B2B *See* Business-to-Business.

B2C *See* Business-to-Consumer.

Boolean operators Special connecting words (that is, AND, OR, and NOT) that indicate the relationship among keywords in a Web search statement.

Business-to-Business A transaction in which a business or other organization orders supplies, equipment, or other goods electronically from another business.

Business-to-Consumer A transaction in which an individual purchases products or services using the Web.

Cache A file of stored Web pages.

Collection A Web site compiled by individuals or organizations to offer information and links to Web sites related to a particular subject.

Control A program included in a Web page that usually enables the page to interact with users. However, some controls can be security risks.

Cookie A small text file stored on your computer by a Web site as you browse the Web; may contain information about your browsing activity on a particular site and/or information you provided to the site.

Document window Area of the browser window that displays the current Web page.

Domain name The part of a URL that indicates the Web site name and extension. For example, in the URL *www.microsoft.com*, the domain name is microsoft.com. *See also* Uniform Resource Locator (URL).

E-commerce *See* Electronic commerce.

Electronic commerce The selling and marketing of goods and services via the Internet.

Electronic publishers Organizations that provide book, magazine, and/or newspaper content online.

E-mail A system used to send and receive messages electronically via an Internet connection; short for electronic mail.

E-mail address The unique name of each e-mail user.

Explorer bar A collection of buttons and controls to help an Internet Explorer user easily maneuver around the Web. The bar is displayed on the left side of the browser window, while the current Web page is displayed on the right side.

Extension The last letters of a domain name that indicate the category to which a Web site belongs. For example, the extension .edu indicates that the Web site is part of the educational domain on the Internet. Also known as top-level domain or global domain.

Favorite The name and address of a Web page stored in the user's collection of favorite Web pages.

Favorites list A feature of Internet Explorer that enables the user to collect and organize the names and addresses of favorite Web pages (or sites) for quick and easy access in the future.

File sharing A technology that enables Internet users to make electronic files available for other users to browse and copy.

Followed link A link that you have previously clicked on a Web page.

Frames Separate windows within the document window, each containing unique information. This feature can display new Web pages in one or more frames while maintaining the same information in other frames.

Global domain The last letters of a domain name that indicate the category a Web site belongs to. For example, the global domain .edu indicates that the Web site is part of the educational domain on the Internet. Also known as a top-level domain or extension.

Go button Opens the URL entered in the Address text box in Internet Explorer.

Home page The initial Web page that loads each time you start a Web browser. The term also refers to the main page of a Web site.

Horizontal scroll bar Enables you to quickly move left and right in a Web page.

Hypertext links, hyperlinks *See* links.

Hypertext Transfer Protocol (HTTP) The communication standard established for the World Wide Web that ensures every computer accessing the World Wide Web is using the same language when sending and receiving Web pages.

IM *See* Instant message.

Index A list of keywords with links to the pages they appear on as compiled by a search engine.

Instant message Messages sent almost instantaneously via an instant messaging system.

Instant messaging A communication system that transmits text messages between individual Internet users almost instantaneously.

Internet A collection of networks that connects computers all over the world using phone lines, fiber optic cables, satellites, and other telecommunications media.

Internet Explorer A Web browser developed by Microsoft that enables users to interact with the World Wide Web.

Intranet A network, or networks, that uses Internet standards but for which access is restricted to the members of a particular group or organization.

Keyword Word entered into a search form to locate content on the Web that contains the word.

Links Web page objects that enable the user to open related Web pages by clicking them. Also known as hyperlinks.

Links toolbar Toolbar that contains a set of buttons that you can customize to quickly access Web pages that you use often.

Location directory Search tool on the Web that allows you to search for resources within a specific geographical region.

Map site A search tool that displays a map showing the location of an address you have entered.

Menu bar Toolbar that displays the names of the menus that contain commands. Clicking a menu name on the menu bar displays a list of commands from which you can choose.

Message board An online forum that allows reading and posting of messages on a variety of subjects by a limited audience of Internet users, such as employees of an organization or members of a group.

Metasearch engine A Web page offering a single form for querying multiple search engine indices simultaneously when searching the Web based on keywords or phrases.

Metasearch tool *See* Metasearch engine.

Navigation bar A set of links running down the left or right side or across the top of a Web page that enables you to efficiently find the information you're looking for on a Web site.

Network Two or more computers connected together to share data.

Newsgroups Online forums where users can read and post messages on a variety of subjects.

Offline The status of not being connected to the Web.

Outlook Express A combined e-mail program and newsgroup reader that allows the user to send, receive, and manage messages, and participate in newsgroup discussions.

Path The text in a URL after the top-level domain.

Portal A Web site that provides a centralized (and potentially customized) set of options for using the Web.

Progress bar Center box on the Status bar that visually indicates the status of a Web page's loading process by filling in with a blue bar.

Refreshing Reloading the Web page displayed in the browser window, to ensure that you see the most recent version of a Web page.

Relevancy scores Ratings of how close search results match a search engine query.

Script A program included in a Web page that usually enables the page to interact with users. However, some scripts can be security risks.

Scroll box A rectangular-shaped control, located in the vertical and horizontal scroll bars, that lets the user quickly move through a long document and indicates the relative position in the document.

Search engine A Web site that lets you specify keywords or phrases to retrieve a list of links to pages on the Web that contain matching information.

Security risks Potential dangers when browsing the Web. Categories of security risks include data confidentiality, computer safety, and personal anonymity.

Spider A computer program used by search engines to index the contents of Web pages at each site as it travels from one site to another.

Sponsored link A valid match to a search engine query that's given prominence on the results page because of advertising payments to the search engine.

Standard Buttons toolbar Toolbar that contains icons that function as shortcuts to frequently used Internet Explorer menu commands.

Status bar Displays important information about the current operation, such as the percentage loaded of a Web page's layout and graphics.

Status indicator Indicates whether or not a Web page is loading in the document window. The indicator becomes animated as a new page is loading; when it stops moving, the page loading process is completed.

Subject directory A list of links to general information topics, arranged alphabetically to facilitate browsing.

Title bar Displays the title of the current Web page at the top of the program window.

Top-level domain The last letters of a domain name that indicate the category a Web site belongs to. For example, the top-level domain .edu indicates that the Web site is part of the educational domain on the Internet. Also known as global domain or extension.

Unfollowed link A link that you have not previously clicked on a Web page.

Uniform Resource Locator (URL) Unique string of text that identifies the location of a Web page on the World Wide Web. Also known as a Web address.

Usenet *See* Newsgroups.

Vertical scroll bar Enables you to quickly move up and down in a Web page.

Web *See* World Wide Web.

Web address Unique string of text that identifies the location of a Web page on the World Wide Web. Also known as a Uniform Resource Locator (URL).

Web browser Computer program that enables users to find, view, and interact with Web sites on the World Wide Web. Web browsers offer easy-to-use point and click environments to quickly access information on the Web.

Web page A specially formatted file designed to be viewed by anyone with access to the World Wide Web via a Web browser. Web pages typically include text, graphics, and links to other Web pages, and may also include sound and video clips.

Web server A computer or a network of computers that stores Web pages and makes them available on the Web.

Web site A collection of linked Web pages that has a common theme or focus.

Web zine An online-only news or information outlet; short for Web magazine.

World Wide Web (WWW) A huge collection of Internet documents called Web pages that use a consistent format for easy accessibility. *See also* Web page.

Index

Index

My Yahoo!
  customized home page, D-15
  home page, D-15

►N

navigating. *See also* Back button;
  Forward button
  backward and forward, B-8–9
navigation bar, described, B-14
network, defined, A-2
newsgroups, described, A-2
New York Times
  article on Web site, D-9
  home page, D-9

►O

offline viewing, B-13
online help. *See also* help
  characteristics of, D-2
  exploring, D-16–18
  online shopping. *See also*
    electronic commerce
  defined, C-3
Options button, described, A-15
Outlook Express, features, A-4

►P

path, defined, B-4
people finders, defined, C-3
person, searching by, C-14–15
personal anonymity, B-16

portals
  defined, D-2, D-14
  exploring, D-14–15
powells.com
  home page, D-5
  shopping cart page, D-5
Print button, described, A-11
Print dialog box, A-17
Print Preview window, A-17
Printing
  options, A-16
  help topic, A-17
  Web page, A-16–17
Privacy tab, B-17
progress bar function, A-8

►R

Refresh button, described, A-11
Refreshing, described, A-10
Related Links, C-3

►S

Salon.com, home page, D-9
scripts, defined, B-16
scroll bar
  horizontal, A-8
  vertical, A-8
scrolling, through Web page,
  A-12–13
Search button, described, A-11
search engine. *See also*
  metasearch engine
  defined, C-3, C-6
Search Engine Watch, C-11

search methods
  Boolean operators and, C-7
  strategies for, C-3
  understanding, C-2–3
Search tab, described, A-15
searching. *See also* metasearching
  by collection, C-10–11
  by content, C-6–7
  by location, C-12–13
  by merchandise, C-16–17
  by person, C-14–15
  by subject, C-4–5
  tools for, C-3
security risks, discussed, B-16–17
Security Settings dialog box, B-17
server. *See* Web server
Shortcuts, for Favorites, B-12–13
Show button, described, A-15
SOC. *See* Student Online
  Companion
spider, defined, C-6
Standard Buttons toolbar,
  described, A-8
Start menu, starting Internet
  Explorer 6, A-6–7
starting Internet Explorer 6, A-6–7
status bar, function, A-8
status indicator, page loading
  indication by, A-8
Stop button, described, A-11
Student Online Companion (SOC)
  described, A-6
  tip for using, B-6
subject, searching by, C-4–5
subject directory
  alphabetical and hierarchical
    structure of, C-5
  defined, C-3, C-4